CW01522631

Hope Amongst the Chaos

'Kupilira' is the pseudonym of an amazing daughter of God.

Hope Amongst the Chaos

by

Kupilira

Jem Authors Agency

Published in the United Kingdom by Jem Authors Agency

First printed January 2024

Content copyright © Kupilira 2024

Design copyright © Jem Authors Agency 2024

This edition © Jem Authors Agency 2024

A CIP record of this book is available from the British Library.

ISBN: 979-887-384-1943

www.jemauthorsagency.com

"I can't change the past, but I am determined to start a new chapter in my life. This time, live it well. The past has taught me a lot. It has given me great survival tools for the future. I'm not broken; I'm still standing. And I'm not planning on going down but up. And yes, I can live the life I desire."

Kupilira, May 2020

One thing I ask from the Lord, this only do I seek; that I may dwell in the house of the Lord all the days of my life, to gaze on the beauty of the Lord and to seek him in his temple.

(Psalm 27: 4)

Contents

My story

Dare to be vulnerable.
Be me.
Laugh a lot.
Love like never before.
I am worthy.
Write my own first love story.
Embrace being different.
Be kind.
I am enough.
Appreciate today.
Venture out into the world.
Be free.
Try something new.
Be humble.
Smile.
Be courageous.
Fall in love.
Sing a new song.
Care.
Do my best.
Be open-minded.

Foreword

I am a living testimony of the goodness of God. He has rescued me from a dark and painful past. A few years ago, a couple of people prayed with me and said that one day I would write a book. I laughed, a bit like Sarah when the angels told Abraham that his wife would bear a child **(Genesis 18: 9-15)**.

In 2019 I visited Israel. That was the beginning of my journey to walking into freedom and away from my past traumas. Something *so* significant happened there. For years I had prayed and asked God that He would bang my head against a wall so that one day I'd wake up and not remember the horrible past.

The Lord works in much mightier and more beautiful ways than that, and He instead met me when I was being re-dedicated at the River Jordan. God *completely* healed me from the past. I remember thinking that it would come back, I had lived under the weight of grief, pain and trauma all my life and I was sure it would return. But it was gone. Suddenly, I was able to talk about the past without feeling sick. I still am. I have been able to forgive and let go. I began to experience what it is like to walk in freedom, having laid all my burdens at the feet of Jesus **(Matthew 11: 28-29, Psalm 55: 22)**. I had tried in my own strength for years to forgive but had never been able to truly do it, but that day it all changed.

As a result of my heart and body being so wounded, it seemed impossible that I would ever be free from the pain, but I realised that I couldn't do it by myself. I then fully surrendered to God. For years I cried myself to sleep, choking on the pain and grief. The day before I was healed, I remember crying to God asking Him to help me. I was drowning and needed a miracle, it felt like I could no longer go on.

I asked God to take the pain away.

Satan had tried to be the victor over my life, but Jesus was the champion. Even when I have been distant from God, He has always been there to carry me through. He carried me when I couldn't walk, held my hand and pulled me along when I was too weak to walk by myself, loved me when I couldn't love myself and waited for me when I said I'd had enough **(Isaiah 46: 4)**.

For years I sang very sad songs – one of them was:

Ndifuna kuti ndikuwoneni. Nyali yazima yiwalitseni dada?
(I want to see your face again Lord, the light has gone out.
Will you light it again Father?)

This song spoke so clearly and deeply into how I was feeling and where I was at, until God healed me.

Just a few nights after I returned from Israel, I woke at three in the morning, and the words 'hope amongst the chaos' came to me. Even though I was half asleep, I felt strongly in my spirit that I needed to write the words down and it was going to be a title of something, but I didn't know what it was.

During the lockdown in May 2020, I was led by the Lord into a forty-day fast. On the eighth day of my fast, I woke at about three thirty in the morning with a strong feeling from the Lord that I needed to start writing my story, so I grabbed a pen and some paper and started writing. Wishing just a few hours, I had journalled so much, it was like my memories were being downloaded supernaturally.

It has been an incredibly painful but fulfilling journey, writing about my past. I have been able to revisit things I had buried away and deal with them. I can see clearly that God's hand was holding me so close, He was always there protecting me from the evil one. Satan's plans were to devour me, but God protected and championed me **(Deuteronomy 31: 6)**.

Thanks to the grace and love of God, I have learnt contentment and to love myself. I know that I am loved by God for who I am, not what I can be. I am enough. I will sing this truth over me again and again like a song – because of Jesus I can sing and dance, because of Jesus I can walk in freedom. I am overwhelmed by God's goodness. All my shame is gone **(Isaiah 43: 19)**. The old is gone, I choose to leave the past behind and look to the future and the certain hope.

Tetelestai.

Growing up with Grandma

I was born in a tiny village in a country in southern Africa. My mother left me at a very young age, so I was raised by my grandma. Mom and Dad were married but only lived together for a short time and when I was just a few months old they separated. Dad had another wife, he had separated from her, but they were still legally married and one day, his ex-wife came back on the scene and she caused a lot of problems for Mom. People say that she was a volatile lady. Mom didn't want to share a husband, so she left, and when she did, she left me. This really broke my dad's heart; he loved my mom so much. However, the family of my dad's ex-wife persuaded him to re-marry his ex because they had children together. In my culture there was and still is a strong family persuasion for a man to remain married to his wife once they have children because a single mother is shunned culturally – a man won't want to marry a woman if she already has a child, and if she has more than one there is almost no hope for her.

Mom had to get married again but it wasn't easy because she had a child. Her second marriage didn't work out either, so she returned home with a baby boy, my half-brother. I don't have a memory of Mom's return as I was only two years old, but I remember growing up with my little brother from the age of about three. After Mom returned home, she got remarried again to her third husband, and she is still with him. I was about three years old, and my brother would have been about one, so I really don't remember her being around or leaving us. We had to stop breastfeeding at an early age and just ate regular food, so it would have been fine for my brother to have been about one when Mom remarried.

Grandma lived in a house in a village in the hills, with only three other houses around. There were acres of land around it. The other three houses belonged to a family friend of Grandma's. One of the brothers took pity on Grandma after she left her husband – she became 'mad' and lived in the mountains before I was born. This brother is somehow related to Grandma, so he offered her a piece of land to build her house there and this helped her to leave the mountains and get well. By the time I was born, she had recovered from her mental illness – in Africa, they just called her a 'mad' person.

I have really fond memories of singing and dancing in the rain with my little brother. We danced in the rain on a regular basis! It rained a lot, so our region was very green. We would hold hands with other children in the village and dance in a circle. One of the songs we used to sing was this...

Mwezi wuwale tisewele timbe.
Asikana akugwila tchito.
(Let the moon come out, let's play and sing.
Girls are working hard.)

14

I loved the smell of the soil when it rained, and the smell of ripe mangoes and bananas. Grandma's house, like the others, was made of mud and had a grass roof. There were only two small rooms inside – one for storing things like food, and the other for sleeping in. So, we all slept together, the three of us, on a mat on the floor. We didn't have a good blanket, so in the cold weather we were really cold at night.

I can remember Grandma telling us stories almost every night as we sat around the fire. We cooked outside under the stars. Me and my little brother would try to count the stars for ages! We would be telling Grandma that the stars were falling, and we would count them until we were exhausted and then we would go to bed. We stayed around the fire for as long as we could to stay warm. Sometimes Grandma would make a fire inside the house if it was too cold, and she would sleep next to it to keep watch to make sure the house didn't catch fire. It was really dangerous, but sometimes it got so cold at night in our village.

My grandma was a very smartly dressed lady and she always wore bright, beautiful colours. My little brother had such a beautiful big smile that I always adored, and it made me happy to see him laughing and smiling. Dancing was our escape from chores; it gave us a break from it. I would have been working at home right from the age of one – as soon as you can walk you are taught a few things, like carrying water in a small bottle or carrying a piece of firewood and helping around the house when the grown-ups were working. They would always give us a little something to do.

We were very poor, so as children we had to work very hard to help Grandma. We worked in the fields growing maize and vegetables. We would pound the maize, fetch water and wood from miles away carrying it on our head. Some days we would go to bed on an empty stomach. Grandma would boil some water for us to drink to keep us going through the night, and she did the same thing in the morning just to soothe our hurting stomachs. We didn't have many clothes so Grandma would wash our clothes at night and just let us go to bed with nothing on so that the clothes could dry during the night, ready for the next day. I didn't know anything about underwear until I was about eight years old so until that age, I didn't wear pants. Whenever I go back to Africa now, I always carry huge bags of pants for the village people, and my mom's daughter. During harvest time, it was like Christmas for us. If the crops had done well that season, we were able to sell them and make enough money for the school fees and have enough left for food. But this was sadly very rare.

We were often kicked out of school because Grandma couldn't afford the fees – she just didn't have the money to pay for it each term. The school we went to was big, and many children from different villages would go there. My class was one of the many which was held under a tree outside because of the lack of classrooms inside. The teachers would write on a small free-standing blackboard. Sadly, nothing much has changed since then. Poverty still has a hold on that part of Africa. Children are happy and jolly most of the time, and I remember as a child we just had to get on with things. I guess you don't have anything to compare it to; you know life is tough, but you have to survive.

On top of all the jobs we were doing at home, we also worked for Grandma's brother who lived next door to us. He would come to our house to wake us up at four in the morning to go and prepare fresh tobacco ready for drying. We had to put a thread through the leaves to make a long line of tobacco and then hang it up to dry. We would be doing this from four in the morning through to six-thirty at which point we would go home for a quick wash and to grab some hot water that Grandma had prepared for us to drink before rushing to school. After the tobacco harvest, Grandma's brother would go to the city and sell it all. He would return home with bags of clothes and shoes for his children and grandchildren. My brother and I would just admire from a distance as he handed them items that he had bought. He would give us nothing, but we were expected to work for him every tobacco season, and so that is exactly what we did.

When times were hard, Grandma would send us to my father's family to get some food from them. Their village was not too far from us, it took about twenty minutes to walk there, and so I would walk from my grandma's house to my father's house. My father and his family were more fortunate than us, their house was big with five bedrooms. He travelled to America a lot, so he built his village house based on city houses he saw on his travels, making it out of bricks, iron sheets and cement floors, very different to our mud hut.

This part of my life is where things got even more difficult. Family have told me that I would have been just two years old when I went with my brother to get food and my dad's son, a grown man, first raped me. I don't remember this, but my memory of being raped does begin from about three years old. This became a devastating pattern, and every time we went to my father's family, I would be raped by him. When my little brother was old enough to join me walking to my father's house, he would be told to wait on the veranda while I was taken into a dark room. It became normal, but Grandma kept on sending us back for food. Sometimes he would come to my home and ask Grandma to let me go with him to get some food from my father's fields. Grandma would always let him; she didn't have a problem with it. But every time I was in the hands of that man, I was raped. Sometimes he would grab me as I was walking back from school, drag me into the maize field and do what he wanted. Grandma did find out one day when I came home and couldn't walk properly, but nothing was done. I don't know if it is because we needed the food or because Grandma didn't have the fight in her. Even now, she still doesn't like talking about what happened. When I ask her why she didn't do anything or try and stop it, she just shuts down and I can't continue questioning her. I heard when I was older that my dad's son died in prison – he was put in prison for raping a young girl and giving her AIDS.

During the time my father's son was abusing me, my uncle who is related to Grandma would also join in. He would see me going to the river by myself and he would follow me. He too abused me over a number of years. Although he is still alive, he is very ill with AIDS. He is treated well among my family and respected by them, even though they know what he did to me. But he is just another monster to me. I have forgiven him, but I can't relate to him or call him my uncle.

The reason I have been able to forgive my uncles is because Jesus tells me to forgive those who have hurt us. The process of forgiving them took a long time. I had nightmares and suffered trauma for many years because of what happened to me, but some verses from the Bible carried me through:

Cast your cares on the Lord and He will sustain you,
He will never let the righteous be shaken.
(Psalm 55: 22)

Come to me, all You who are weary and burdened and I will give you rest. Take my yoke upon you and learn from me, for I am gentle and humble in heart, and you will find rest for your souls. For my yoke is easy and my burden is light.
(Matthew 11: 28-29)

Even on those days when I didn't want to get up, I remembered these verses and kept going. Most days I sang them with tears running down my face; a song that I learned at Sunday school in Africa.

Cast your burdens onto Jesus
For He cares for you.

It had been such a heavy burden to carry; there was so much grief and so much pain. I was a prisoner to it all, but I had to let go and forgive so that I could be free. Only God could have made this happen, only God is able to take away that much pain. In 2019 when I went to Israel, it was such a significant time for me. I was rededicated and there was a sudden release of *all* the pain that I had been carrying for years. God had healed me. As I stand today, I am free from it all because of Christ. He took away my pain, I feel liberated, no longer a prisoner and I thank God for this.

My Grandad

My dad's father, my grandad, divorced my grandmother and married another woman but they stayed in the same village. I am told that when I was born, he instantly bonded with me. Although I didn't see him often, when I did, we had the best time together.

He had lots of animals and acres of land and worked very hard in the fields. He was a gentleman who loved life. He never seemed to want more. He looked quite content with what he had but worked hard for it. I would visit him once in a while or he would come for me at my grandma's house. I still remember the joy and the excitement I had when he one day invited me to visit him at his house. When I got there with my little brother, he gave me two ducks to keep – a female and a male. When the ducks had ducklings and eggs, we would sell them to help me with our school fees.

Although I didn't spend a lot of time with Grandad, I have such fond memories of him. When we did spend time together, we had such a wonderful time. He created so many beautiful memories that I hold dearly close to my heart. He taught me so many things – how to fish, how to hunt rabbits and birds. Grandad also taught me to hunt and collect honey from the forest. He showed me which mushrooms were okay to eat and which ones to avoid. He taught me to milk the cows without all the fancy machines we have nowadays.

Oh, I had such wonderful adventures with Grandad. We would go to the river and find a spot where we thought there would be a lot of fish. We would block the water by mashing up a plant that made the fish a little drowsy, then we would use bamboo canes to spear the fish. Grandad was very good at it but I missed quite a few times. I think it was because I would be staring at the fish jumping up and down thinking they would not move so fast, but I was so wrong because that plant didn't keep them drowsy for too long. I was so happy if I managed to get one though because I saw how proud Grandad was when I did get one. Sometimes I would use a T-shirt or any cloth material that we had to catch the fish.

We would also go into the woods and look for honeycombs. If we found one in a tree, we would make smoke under the tree with special green leaves. Grandad knew which leaves to pick, there were some that were less harmful to the bees, and then he would climb the tree and collect the honey. I loved it when he would drop some down for me to eat. Most of the time I came so close to putting the honeycomb in my mouth with the bees still on it, but Grandad was so quick at reminding me not to do that.

He also taught me how to make a slingshot from rubber, most of the time we would get it from an old wheel from a bike. We would use a piece of Y-shaped wood to make the slingshot which we used for hunting birds, and we made traps in the jungle to catch rabbits. My favourite thing was when we had finished the hard work of hunting, we would go to his house and milk the cows for a nice drink of fresh milk. It was a little strong for me but Shhh! Grandad thought it was my favourite. Sadly, my grandad passed away when I was in the orphanage. He was a great man.

Grandchildren are the crown of the aged,
and the glory of children is their fathers.
(Proverbs 17: 6)

My Father

When I was five years old, a man came to my house. It was my father. This was the first time I had seen him, but I am told that he would visit often. He had come to ask Grandma if he could take me to go and live with him in the city. Grandma agreed so I went with him. My dad had moved to the city with his ex-wife shortly after my mum left him and they re-married. I didn't know what to expect, but I was happy to know that I had a father. When we got to the city, things seemed good. My father took me shopping a few days after we arrived and bought me some lovely clothes and a pair of shoes which I only wore as a treat. It was the first time I had owned a pair of shoes so I walked very carefully when I was wearing them.

Within weeks of arriving in the city, my father had to go back to work. I discovered then that he had to work away quite often and would be gone for weeks, sometimes months at a time, and this time he was going away for a few months. When he was gone, I realised that although my father wanted me in the city with him, his wife and children didn't. Most days they wouldn't feed me. One of his sons would beat me for no reason. Dad's wife would find a reason to beat me with a stick. It was horrendous. The physical and mental abuse became so severe that I remember longing to turn into a bird so that I could fly away, back to my home village.

I remember one day I got very sick – my dad had been gone for quite a long time. My grandma came to visit me, she had come to the city to visit someone she knew and decided she would come and visit me whilst she was there. When she arrived, she found me lying on a mat fighting malaria, and malnourished, not having been fed for days. When she asked my dad's children what was going on, they made up excuses saying that I had lost so much weight because I was so sick with malaria and that I had only been 'this' ill the day she visited. I wanted to tell her the truth, but I knew there would be consequences once she had gone. I also knew that she couldn't take me back with her without my dad being around and giving permission even if she found out about the abuse. My grandma chatted with me and told me how my brother was doing, but this only made me miss him even more. When she was saying goodbye I think she knew that I was being abused, but because she couldn't do anything without my dad there and I couldn't tell her that I was suffering, she left for the village.

When my dad returned home, he noticed my weight loss. He asked around to try and find out what had been going on when he was gone. He couldn't ask me, but neighbours started telling him that I was being abused by his wife and children. He knew that I would be in trouble when he was gone again, so he started feeding me at five in the morning before anyone else in the house was awake. He would get up before five and prepare food for us both – it was *so* lovely to just sit with him and eat together. I felt protected. Nothing could touch me and nobody could hurt me. I was invisible to them when Dad was around. He made sure that he spent as much time with me as possible when he was home. Dad loved to dance so we danced a lot together, he would dance with me before work, and we would dance again after work. I remember the first time he put the radio on, I was absolutely amazed by it! I had never seen a radio before. I thought that people had shrunk into tiny little humans to fit inside so that they could speak on the radio. I was so curious that one day, when Dad had gone to work, I smashed it on the floor because I wanted to see the little people. Oh, it makes me laugh to think of it now! When Dad came home, instead of being angry with me, I think he felt sad – his other children understood how it worked but I didn't; I hadn't been taught. So, he sat me down and explained how the radio worked. He loved music, so at weekends he would blast out all sorts of music and we would dance. He wanted so much for my stepmum and his other children to join in, but I think they just struggled to relate to me as part of their family. I don't believe that Dad was perfect and didn't have any flaws, but I know he wanted to make things right for me and his family. Sadly though, this wasn't going to happen.

Within months of being with Dad, just before I was six, he had to go away again. The abuse continued at home as soon as he left. There was nothing anyone could have done to stop it. After some time, Dad returned home but he was very sick, so he had to go to the hospital. He got admitted to the city hospital and stayed there for a while. One day, some men who worked for Dad came to our house in the night to take me and my dad's children back to the village. They said that we had to go to our home village as Dad was so unwell. They also told us that he would come for us when he got better. The men packed up all the furniture in the house. I didn't even ask them why we were taking everything if Dad was coming back for us when he got better, I guess as a child I just trusted the grown-ups. After everything was packed, we left for the village. We travelled all night. Not long after we arrived in the village, my father and his wife followed us, but my dad was very sick with HIV and Aids. He looked so sick and so unlike my dad that I remember being afraid and feeling scared to sit next to him. My dad's children started at the school in the village, but I was so confused and afraid of what was happening with him that I didn't go to school. Instead, I sat with him. Every day.

I remember Grandma would bring my little brother with her to see me every day as well. With the help of Grandma, Dad encouraged me to spend more time with him and to just sit next to him. Some days I would cry, telling him to get better so that we could dance again. I would sing his favourite song to him – *Nyaphiri wayendekela ndi kayimayima.* I didn't have much to say to him, but he would constantly tell me how much he loved me, and that he was sorry for not being there from the start. One thing that has always stuck with me was his confidence in God. He would always tell me that God would look after me and that I had nothing to worry about because God would always be there for me. I had been to Sunday School and Grandma talked about God looking after us a lot when we were younger, so when Dad said that God would take care of me, I believed him and felt confident that He would. I imagined someone bigger and greater who looked after the Heavens and Earth. Grandma had told me that this God has power to create Heaven and Earth and humankind, so he was the King of everything. I knew in my heart that a God like this was capable of looking after me.

I think I knew that things were not good with Dad when he asked the church choir to come and sing in his room each day. Although I knew things were not great, I didn't understand death, so I was just waiting for him to get better. One day, he called me to sit next to him. He held my hand for a long time that day. He chatted with me for a little while, then he turned to look at me and said, "God has got you". He then asked the choir to sing 'Amazing Grace' and with my hand in his, Dad passed away. Some of the choir members had noticed that he was gone so they separated my hand from his and took me outside of the house.

Soon after I heard people crying and somehow I knew that I would never see him again.

I felt so lonely and lost. So many people came to the funeral as my dad was a very well-known and well-loved man in the region. I don't remember anyone comforting me, but I do remember being asked to fetch water for the funeral visitors. Everything was just a fog that day. I had only just started getting to know this man, my father, and to be torn apart so quickly didn't make sense. What's more it didn't seem fair. I didn't understand. I questioned God's love. I didn't understand why he would take from me the only person that I felt safe with. I was so confused about the love of God. I remember asking someone when I was putting the soil on top of Dad's coffin, "why did God take Dad away from me? Doesn't he care about me? Who is going to look after me now?", and they answered me saying that God did not want to hurt me, but he had taken Dad into a better place because he had been very sick and in a lot of pain, and now he was with God he was no longer suffering. To hear that Dad was no longer in pain comforted me a little but it didn't take away the sadness and the confusion I was feeling. It wasn't until I was ten years old when I gave my life to Jesus that I began to understand a little more about God's love, and that He didn't take my dad to hurt me. One day I remembered the song Dad sang before he took his last breath – *Chisomo Chodabwisacho (Amazing Grace)*. It was like someone put a light on! I began to cry and laugh at the same time as if I was crazy, but I wasn't going mad. God had revealed to me that it was His amazing grace that had saved Dad. Dad was not living a Christ-centred life after Mom left and he ended up getting HIV and Aids, *but* in the midst of this sickness and trial he found Christ again. So, I was relieved that I would one day see him again, but just not yet. Even though I missed him terribly I began to thank God for Dad's life, even to this day I continue to thank God that he found God's love and forgiveness again. For that I'm forever grateful.

After the burial, my stepmum announced that she was returning back to the city with her children, but that she wasn't taking me with her. I call it a blessing because I don't know if I would have survived if I had gone with them. A woman who knew my father offered to look after me, so I went with her, further north in my country. Things were good. But soon after, her son and another family member arrived to stay for good. They were introduced to me as my uncles, so I would call them 'uncle'. Straight after their arrival they started raping me. They would take turns. One would come one night, the other the following night. If they gave me a notebook for school, I knew that I would be raped that night. But there was nothing I could do about it. Just under a year of being there, my dad's son arrived. My dad's wife, his mother, had passed away, so he decided to come and join me because the lady I was living with was a very good friend of my father. I used to call her 'Grandma' and her husband 'Grandad' because they were about the same age as my grandma. They were financially comfortable so my dad's son knew that he would be looked after. When he arrived they couldn't turn him away, he had nowhere else to go now his mother had passed away. During that time, he became very abusive towards me again and began beating me up like he used to in the city. He would call friends of his to throw stones at me every time I went to fetch some water from the river. Meanwhile, my 'uncles' continued to sexually abuse me. I heard that one of my uncles passed away a few years ago with HIV and Aids, and the other one is very sick with Aids. It is an absolute miracle that I am here at the age of thirty-two years old and perfectly well. Dad was right – God protects me and He has kept me free from sickness.

For it is by grace you have been saved,
through faith and this is not from yourselves,
it is the gift of God.
(Ephesians 2: 8)

My Mother

When I was seven and a half years old, I heard that my mom had been involved in an accident – her house had burned down whilst she was inside. She was living in a thatched house and lit a paraffin lamp which blew up on her and the whole roof fell in on top of her causing severe burns. Someone knew where she was, so I left where I was living with one of my uncles and his sister to return to my home village so that someone could take me to her. I knew that my uncle wouldn't hurt me on the way because we were with his sister, and I also remember feeling so relieved that I was getting away from my dad's son beating me. I don't understand why but the beating used to hurt me more. We left first thing in the morning to get to the nearest bus depot, it took us about five hours to walk there. I was tired and hungry, with no shoes on my feet so they were in agony. The only time I remember wearing shoes was when my dad bought me a pair in the city. So, although walking bare foot was normal for me, it didn't stop the blisters from coming up.

The coach was travelling overnight, so we got to my home village the morning of the following day. My uncle and his sister dropped me off at the bus depot in my home village and they carried on with their journey to their village – it was the next stop. I wasn't too far from my mother's village, where my little brother was. I remember being able to see the houses from the depot. My dad's house was only a few minutes from where I was, but I decided to run to my grandma's village because I was scared that my father's son might still be around at the house, and I didn't want to put myself in danger of being raped so I ran and kept going until I got to Grandma's house.

When I got to my mother's village, I found my little brother and my mom's brother who I had never met before. He lived in another country, but had come back after hearing about the accident. Grandma had already gone to the hospital to look after Mom, so my little brother was left at home alone, but Grandma's brother and family kept an eye on him. We were so happy to see each other again! I had brought a few things with me. One of them was a pair of girl's trousers which he still talks about now. He had not owned or worn a pair of trousers until this point; he only had shorts. He was so happy and couldn't wait to put on the trousers. We danced so much to celebrate our reunion.

That evening, my mom's brother offered to take me to see Mom, and the next day we left for the hospital. My brother stayed at home, I had brought a few things with me to keep him going for a while – rice, maize flour, beans, soap, and Vaseline for the skin problems he had. The hospital was a few hours away, so it was another long journey for me. When we got to the hospital, we met Grandma outside. She took us to where Mom was. I didn't know what to expect, but when we got to her, I remember seeing a pink-skinned body lying in a see-through box. It completely freaked me out, so much so that I ran away and went outside. The doctor followed me and then Grandma came, and we waited for my mom's brother to join us. I honestly thought I had seen a ghost. But that was my mom. She had suffered from severe burns and was in a coma for a long time. I didn't want to go back inside. We stayed overnight at a relative's house, just across the road from the hospital. The next morning, we left for my home village. That was the first time I had seen my mom for a long time.

My mother's brother stayed with us for a few days before he returned home, and then sadly he passed away shortly after that. I didn't return to see Mom; the next time I saw her I was seventeen. Grandma continued to visit my mom, and I stayed in the village to look after my brother while we waited for Grandma to return home. We continued to work for Grandma's brother on the tobacco farm. One thing I had learned by then was to survive, so I made every effort to make sure that my brother was okay, no matter what the cost would be. I had to look after him. Sometimes, Grandma's brother and his family would give us food, but most of the time, we had to fetch food for ourselves. We would climb mango and papaya trees to eat the fruit and stay up there eating up to the point where our stomachs felt like they would burst... I still remember the taste of fresh mangoes – absolutely delicious!

After some time, Grandma returned to the village. Mom recovered and went back to her home with her husband. It was good to see Grandma again. Life carried on, but our struggle to find food didn't end. I remember Grandma praying a lot and I saw God answer – like the times she would pray for food, and someone would visit us that very day bringing us a bowl of maize flour and a chicken with it. That food parcel would keep us going for quite a few days. I also started going to school again with my brother. We enjoyed it, partly because it was our escape from the house chores! We were generally happy children, but I was incredibly protective over my little brother. I didn't mind people hurting me, but if anyone did anything to him, I would take them on! We did everything together – we climbed trees, we went sliding down the hills on a banana leaf, we made flip flops from a tree that has long flat-looking fruits. We would put string through them to make them look like flip-flops. Although we worked very hard, we played a lot together.

The Orphanage

One day, Grandma asked me to go to my dad's family to pick up some food. I didn't even think about my dad's son and what he might do to me, and I went along happily after school. However, this time I was alone. My brother went back home with our friends. It's normal for children to walk to school and back by themselves from the age of about three. When I got to my dad's family, his son wasn't there so I stayed a bit longer and chatted to my dad's mother. While I was there, a light blue van appeared outside. A man and a woman came and introduced themselves to me, she said she was my aunty. I later found out she was my dad's sister who I had never met before. She was very fortunate and lived a very good life in the city. The man was a village director from an orphanage there. They gave me and my dad's three children some bread to eat and Fanta to drink. My dad's son had returned to the village shortly after I had left, so he was there with me when the van arrived. My aunty asked us to get in the van and we were taken away. It completely broke me leaving my brother again without saying goodbye. It wrecked me. I was only eight years old, but it felt like something died in me that day.

It was a long drive. We arrived at the orphanage at about midnight. We were in the back of the van, not knowing or seeing where we were going. After we had settled in and been there for a couple of hours, my aunty left and went back to her house which was about an hour away from the orphanage. The orphanage was well-equipped – the house was amazing; they were very European-looking buildings.

The next morning, we were taken to the office to register our names. My dad's children denied that we were related, but the village father registered us all under my father's name. I think he knew that they were acting out of unkindness, and he was very kind towards me. The orphanage had about five hundred children and I was put in house number eight with my dad's children. They continued bullying me, but I got on so well with the village father that I didn't feel too alone. He would invite me to his family home to eat with him, his wife and their children. This was not the normal thing to be happening, but he did it for me. He would sometimes take me to church with his family. They were just nice people. Going to their house was one of the best things ever. I felt like I mattered. I felt like I was somebody. I felt that I wasn't a waste of peoples' time. When I was at his family home, we played *phada* with his children. We would draw boxes on the floor, and we had to jump into them, making sure we didn't step on the line – a bit like 'hopscotch' that is played in the UK.

Sadly, after just a year and a half of being in the orphanage, the village father got very sick and quickly passed away. His wife and children then had to move out of the orphanage house and I never saw them again. Just a few weeks after he died, we got a new village director to take over and he moved in with his family. When he got introduced to us, I remember the children saying that they did not like him. One of the first things the new village director said to us was that his children were very lucky to have him, and we were not as lucky because our parents had died of HIV/ Aids and that was why we were orphans. Although he might have meant that well, it was painful to hear – I really didn't like being called an orphan. He was also a harsh man, the way he spoke was incredibly undermining of everyone, which I didn't like. I know that the lady in charge of education didn't like him either along with many others, as he was such an arrogant man.

Although I was only nine and a half years old, I didn't remain silent about the corruption I saw going on in the orphanage – it was so bad! When sponsors or anyone else visited the orphanage, I would tell them everything I knew that was going on. The village director and his team didn't like this, but it didn't stop me. I wanted people to know the good and the bad. At home things weren't going well either. In each house, there were twelve children and one mother and a day auntie. The day auntie would come in each morning and go home at night. Every week, we would have a different auntie, and some I got on well with but others I didn't. My mother in the orphanage didn't like me and I seemed to only ever be in her good books if I did *all* the work she had given me. I think the main reason I didn't get on with the house mother was because I found bottles of Fanta and Coca-Cola hidden under her bed, and of course I challenged her and asked why we didn't get to drink them – she said it was only for grown-ups. This kind of thing was happening in every house. Mothers bought Coke and Fanta for themselves, and we were not allowed to drink it, *but* when their own blood children visited them, they would give them these drinks. I found this really difficult to accept. I guess she didn't like anyone rising up to her or questioning her intentions. This incident happened right at the beginning of my arrival at the orphanage, so we didn't start the relationship well, and she seemed to favour one of the girls in the house and my dad's children. I've always thought it's maybe because they were obedient and didn't question anything like I did.

I was only eight years old when I arrived at the orphanage but I was the oldest girl in the house, so I was given more responsibilities. I had to make sure that things were done properly, that jobs had been completed in the expected way. We weren't allowed food until we had done all the jobs, and even though now I can see this is unreasonable, at the time it was the norm. It was the rule most (although not all) houses made. The jobs I did included cleaning and polishing the floors until they were shiny. The polish was red, so this had to be done once everyone had gone to bed to avoid polish getting on anyone's clothes. I would still be up until one in the morning sometimes trying to get the job done. And then I had to wake up at four to cook porridge for breakfast. The porridge was made from Soya flour that you had to mix with water and then let it boil for hours before serving. Other jobs were washing all the bedding by hands which had to be done on a big flat stone, making sure that the beds were immaculate. Everything had to be kept super neat and in its place. We had someone come every week to check how clean the houses were kept. It was hard work!

My father's children continued to physically and mentally abuse me, especially his son. When I cooked and served everyone the same, he would want more than all of us. I couldn't have cooked in a bigger pot; I was cooking for fourteen people and still so young that the large pot was already too big for me. I physically wasn't strong enough to use a bigger one. They were huge pots that we used, and big wooden spoons to cook with and I remember cooking *nsima*, a bit like a thick porridge, in them. You needed a lot of energy. To make matters even worse, one of the day aunties moved in permanently and she would support my dad's son. She would agree that he should beat me if I wronged him or answered him back, she would lock doors and let him beat me with a kettle cord, she would say that I was naughty answering back to my big brother. It was so bad and so violent that I used to think he would kill me from beating me so badly. The house mother and auntie were best friends, so they supported each other.

Once a year the orphanage held a celebration, where the founder was remembered. At Christmas, we all celebrated together in a big village hall. We would eat together and have plays going on and people dancing different dances, one of which was called *minoghwe*. During these times of celebration, the mother would buy beautiful princess dresses for the girls to wear, but I would have a 'Grandma-looking' suit made by the village tailor. I watched and admired all the other children's beautiful dresses and it hurt me so much. I didn't have any friends then; I think because I was hurting so much I just kept myself away from other people. I hardly went out after my friendly village father died and most of the time I suffered from terrible headaches. I remember I was put in a school play where I played the part of a bridesmaid. I didn't have anything to wear of course, but there was a girl who let me borrow her dress – it was a beautiful green princess dress. She wasn't from the orphanage; she only came to the school there. I remember when I tried the dress on that I felt so beautiful, I remember the joy in my heart, I was so happy, I felt like a princess! After the show, it was hard to return the dress, but I had to.

Jesus

Over time, I made three best friends. They were a few years older than me, but we became very close. They looked out for me when I was out and about. They loved God and used to run a Friday prayer meeting after school which they started inviting me to, to make sure that I was okay. I was safe with them. They used to tell me that God saw my struggles and that one day He would meet me in my despair. They knew I was hurting. They witnessed what my dad's children and auntie were doing to me, but they couldn't practically do anything about it as they were also children from the orphanage.

The orphanage was closed in; it had a brick wall all around it. We could only see the outside world from one side, but on Sundays we were allowed to go out. We could go to church, or go and see friends. We just had to make sure that we were back in good time, otherwise we would be locked out and get in trouble. Gates would normally be open from eight in the morning, so one

Sunday, I decided to go to Sunday school. When I was there, the teacher began to talk about having a relationship with Jesus and how that gives us hope, that through Jesus, we can have eternal life where there will be no more pain or suffering. Even though I didn't understand much, I knew what he meant. I wanted so much to be in that place of no pain. To me, nothing made sense. But this name Jesus seemed more promising than anything else around me. My father had talked about the goodness of this name Jesus. My grandma had so much faith in this name Jesus. My friends talked about this name Jesus. And now my Sunday school teacher was talking about what I could have through the name of Jesus. So, I gave my life to Jesus when I was ten years old. I was baptised and was able to speak in tongues. There was a sense of belonging, none of it made sense but I felt safe.

The power of Jesus is an incredible thing that one can only testify to if they themselves have experienced it. When I prayed, I felt closer to God, and I was assured that He was watching over me. There was this amazing feeling of peace. When I called on the name of Jesus, everything changed in that one moment. I felt the Holy Spirit surrounding me. I felt safe in His presence. When I called on the name of Jesus, He surely came into the midst of my pain. I felt comforted and I felt loved. I felt that I mattered. I felt that my sins were forgiven. I felt that even though I was not enough, Jesus still cared for me. When I called on the name of Jesus, I felt that I belonged. Even though things didn't always make sense, I knew when I called on the name of Jesus, I would be okay. That name Jesus is the name I seemed to not be able to live without. The name Jesus gave me hope for yesterday, today and forever. That name Jesus was the only name I could trust.

I couldn't afford to miss those Friday prayer meetings, but I didn't always go to church. The more I pressed into prayer, the more I suffered abuse from my dad's son. He would call a group of children to come and watch whilst he was beating me up if I answered him back. The other children would just stand and watch me getting beaten up. He would call me names and tell the other children that I was bleeding like a slaughtered chicken, he said that he heard my mother had been burned in a fire and that she cried like an animal. My heart ached so much with these comments. I wished my dad could have been around to stop it.

When I was eleven years old, I was removed from the house and put into a girl's hostel with five other girls who were much older than me. We were alone in the hostel, but we had a youth leader who lived next door. There were two hostels – one for girls and the other for boys. The youth leader was very close to the village father, so I was unlucky there again.

The girls bullied me so much. They reported every mistake I made, and my punishment was extreme – I wouldn't be given my monthly money for food and other things. In the hostel, we were given money to help teach us independence, so if I didn't get enough money that month, I would run out before I had even started. First, I had to contribute towards food, and this meant other things were simply impossible to get with no money.

I remember using toilet paper for my periods. If my budget for food had run out, I would have to go hungry until the next pay. I would be working in the fields which most of the children did, and they were growing tomatoes and other vegetables, but I was just so weak and hungry.

I wasn't the only one facing these harsh punishments. Most of the children were being punished, but it seemed especially severe towards me. It felt like it was more personal, more than just a punishment to teach me a lesson when I made a mistake. It wasn't a secret either. They would announce who was on 'punishment' that month so that everyone could keep an eye on you, make sure that you were doing what you should be and not doing what you shouldn't. On top of not being given all your monthly money, we were given extra jobs, either in the fields or at home. It was torture.

Over time, I had trained my brain to not feel hungry because there was no other way of finding food in the hostel. There was literally nothing I could have done about it. If any of the other children would help by giving us food, they too would then also get punished. Although I was coping, I was very sad and lifeless most of the time. I missed my little brother so much. Many days, because I felt so awful, I did wonder if Dad would come back for me to take me to where he was.

In the orphanage, there was a lady in charge of education. One day, she stood up for me, which was incredibly courageous! She could have lost her job by doing this. After this, she started inviting me into her home. She lived with her children, and they began to look after me. They would feed me and make sure that no one was watching me go into their home. We became so close, and they would call me their little sister. I began to pray to God more than ever. I just wanted to be a child and be happy, but these moments of happiness were so rare.

I became very sad and it was at this really low point that I could think of no other option than to run away. So, I started planning my escape.

You have searched me, Lord and you know me.
You know when I sit and when I rise, you perceive my thoughts from afar.
You discern my going out and my lying down, you are familiar with all my ways.
Before a word is on my tongue you, Lord, know it completely.
You hem me in behind and before, and you lay your hand upon me.

Such knowledge is too wonderful for me, too lofty for me attain.
Where can I go from your spirit? Where can I flee from your
presence?
If I go up to the heavens, you are there, if I make my bed in the
depths, you are there.
If I rise on the wings of the dawn, if I settle on the far side of the sea
Even there your hand will guide me, your right hand will hold me fast.
(Psalm 139: 1-10)

Great Escape

One day I just decided to leave, even though I hadn't saved up enough money or as much as I had planned to save, I wasn't thinking straight, I just knew I needed to get out of there. It was on a Sunday, so no one questioned me about where I was going. We were allowed to go to church on Sundays, or we could visit a friend if we had any outside of the orphanage. I walked out of the gate with a few other people who were going to church that morning. I was worried about how I was going to get away from them, but I was so determined that I was not going to stay another day in that place. So, when we got to the busy roads, I managed to lose the other children in the crowd of people. I went into town and boarded a bus to a city in the south of the country.

My plan was to get a job there as a house-girl. It was a thriving city, so I knew it wouldn't be a struggle to find a job there. I wanted to work and save up enough money so that I could return to my home village one day. I got to the city in the early evening just

43

as it was starting to get dark outside. Once I got off the bus, I went under a bridge with no idea what my next step would be. As I walked under the bridge it was getting dark, but it was just light enough to see where I was going. I bumped into a guy who was just standing there with a panga knife in his hands. It is a large African knife with a broad blade, much like a machete, and I was shaking with fear, but I held my head high and continued to walk under the bridge. I didn't want him to notice that I was scared of him. I don't know why I thought this way, because I was actually terrified, so much so that I wet myself. But my brave face worked. He didn't come near me. I remember walking so fast, and I could feel my heart beating so hard. I kept on looking over my shoulder to see if he was following me.

Just as I was coming up out of the bridge a minibus pulled up. The driver asked me where I was going at that time of day, noticing how young I was. I told him that I wanted to go to a church called Calvary Family Church – it was the name of the church I attended at the orphanage, and I knew there was one in the city. I guess at this point I had also started to think that it would be a safe place to go as it was getting late.

I didn't have any money left but the bus driver still offered to drop me there as he would be passing by the church on his route. He hoped that it would be the Sunday that the church held their evening prayer sessions but he said he wasn't sure. I got on the bus and he drove off. The minibus was full of people, so I tried to look away as much as possible. I was scared that the orphanage had reported me missing to the police and that people would be out looking for me. I had been gone for nearly the whole day by now, I didn't want to be found after getting this far. The minibus dropped me off by the church which was right by the side of the road.

I was so relieved when I saw the lights and people through the window. The bus driver wished me good luck and drove off. I went into the church and stayed right at the back. The church was packed! The ushers got me a chair and I sat on the end of a row, because I wanted to stay close to the door. I love dancing but during the worship even when I tried to force myself to dance and worship I couldn't. I felt so sad, I really did feel dead inside and all I wanted was for God to either bring my dad back or for God to take me to him. I felt like my body was here, but my soul had died in me, there was such a horrible void feeling inside me. I felt incredibly lost and lonely in the world.

When the evening worship was coming to an end, I became scared and I tried to sneak out quickly. I don't know where I would have gone, but I just needed to get out of there. As I was about to leave the pastor spoke, "there is a young girl in this room going through trials. God wants her to know that He hears her prayers". I got even more scared, so I tried to run out of the church but there were women waiting for me at the door who then took me to the pastor's office. I sat down with these women, and they assured me that I was safe and that all would be well. They were wearing badges so I knew they helped out at church, and they were really kind to me so I felt safe with them. After waiting for a while, the pastor came to see me. He introduced himself and asked who I was. I lied and said my name was Rose and that I came from a town miles away from the orphanage. I told him that I was looking for a housekeeping job to earn some money so that I could go back home to look after my sick grandma.

He didn't seem to want to ask me more questions, instead he gave me some money. Enough for me to get to the town I had mentioned with a little bit extra for the journey. He told me that I was too young to be a house-girl so I must return to my grandma. He asked the church usher boys to take me to the depot and to make sure that I boarded the bus safely. I had just enough time to get the midnight coach, so I got on and spent the night travelling.

When I got to where the orphanage was, I got off the coach and started walking to my aunty's house. She was the one who had initially taken me to the orphanage and even though she never visited me or Dad's children whilst we were in the orphanage, I was really hoping that she would take me in, especially if I told her about all the struggles and problems that I was facing. She had similar aged children to me so I thought she would understand.

On the journey I had wet myself a lot, so I was smelly and wet. I was looking forward to having a wash. When I got to my aunty's house, she welcomed me by shouting at me and telling me that she would stick a stiletto heel in my private parts. She was fuming! I then realised that the orphanage had contacted her, so she already knew that I had run away, but she didn't want to know the reason why. Instead, she told me to wait in the lounge and she went off into her room. Her children came and said hello, but then they quickly departed and went into their rooms too. I don't know if she told them not to wait with me. So, I sat on my own and waited and waited.

The Vision

After a while, I saw the van from the orphanage at the gate. I was broken. I felt devastated that my own aunty would treat me like this! She didn't even give me a chance to have a wash. I was taken back to the orphanage and the village director and youth leaders were furious with me. At the time, I really believed that it would have been better not to have been found at all. I was severely punished because of what I had done.

When I was twelve years old, not long after this incident, I became very sick, and I was taken to the hospital by the village nurse. At the hospital, I was approached by a missionary doctor who had been on his way out of the building but stopped when he saw me in the waiting room. Apparently, I looked very sick. There was a kindness that came from the doctor and he just kept smiling, even as people passed by, he would say hello and spoke with such care. I remember feeling like I could trust him. The village nurse told him what she thought was wrong with me. He decided to stay and do a scan on me. When he found out the results, he asked the nurse to let the orphanage know that he was going to take me to his hospital, which was a couple of hours away from the orphanage.

I needed emergency surgery because he had discovered a tumour growing inside me which was infected, and he was worried that it would burst and poison me. The nurse and I followed the doctor and when we got to the hospital, I was helped to get ready for surgery. Before he started to operate with his team, he prayed for me and I can still remember it... he prayed that God would give me the life that He intended me to have and that I would get well and live a life like a child would. He also prayed for God's will to be fulfilled in my life and that Jesus would be in charge of the surgery. He said, "May you Lord be the surgeon during the operation," and he asked God to perform a miracle and to guide them during the operation. Then, I was put to sleep.

When the surgery was over, I didn't wake up straight away. During the operation, I went to another place, so I didn't expect to wake up at the time they were expecting me to.

In the vision, I saw myself in a coffin made of ice and I was able to see right through it. All around me were beautiful, iced surroundings and it was so peaceful. It looked really cold, but I wasn't cold. I was walking on a path looking where I was going and as I looked a little further ahead, I saw a man wearing a beautiful white robe. His eyes were piercing bright.

I looked up and said to him, "I know you."

He smiled and said, "Come closer, look where the nails went into my feet and see my hands where the nails went."

I looked and saw holes in his feet and hands. With joy, I said to him, "Yes! I know you. You're Jesus."

Then He smiled and said, "Go back little girl."

I didn't know where I was meant to be going, but I woke up coughing and found myself surrounded by the doctor and his missionary team. I told the doctor that I had seen Jesus, and he answered me saying he knew and that he had also seen Him when he was praying for me. After that I was taken back to the ward. I stayed in the hospital for a long time and the kind doctor visited me every time he was at the hospital. He talked a lot about God's love, and he told me that God would do great things in my life.

A few days before I was discharged from the hospital, I began to receive hundreds of letters from a college in the UK. It was so strange because they had never written to me before and I hardly ever got any letters from my sponsors. Some of the children at the orphanage would get a postcard every now and then from sponsors but never more than that, so this abundance of letters was a complete surprise. I was just as shocked as everyone else around me. When I got discharged from the hospital, I went back to the orphanage and after some time I was able to return to school. Things unfortunately didn't change. The mental abuse carried on and, because I had run away, I was watched in everything I did. I wasn't allowed to go to church by myself anymore. I felt like a prisoner.

The following year, I received a letter from a married couple in the UK saying that they were going to come and visit me in the orphanage. The husband worked at the college that had sent me letters when I was in hospital. I was very excited.

When they visited, they also came with the head-girl of the college. We had such a great time together and it really helped me to think of something else and to be distracted. I, along with my dad's children, went for dinner at their guest house one evening, and we visited a few places together. The husband preached a few times at the orphanage college, and the head-girl spoke a few times about the UK. The wife was a bit quieter but we spoke a little to one another. They stayed for two weeks, and then went back to the UK.

Life then carried on as normal for me. After about a year had gone by, I got a letter from the husband and wife inviting me to visit them in the UK. This was every child's dream in the orphanage – I didn't even believe that it was possible! So, when I was fourteen years old my life seemed to change overnight. There was a lot to do, I had to apply for a passport and the orphanage helped me to sort out all the other documents that I needed. It was a miracle, but I had no time to think about how it had happened, I was just so happy!

The Lord will pour out His spirit
And it shall come to pass afterward, that I will pour out my Spirit on all flesh; your sons and your daughters shall prophesy,
your old men shall dream dreams,
and your young men shall see visions.
(Joel 2: 28)

Living the Dream

A couple of months later I flew to England by myself. I was given instructions to follow so I wasn't feeling scared and getting out of the orphanage was better than anything else at the time, so I remember just feeling very excited about the trip. I was told that I would know when I reached England because it would be cold, especially in the North, and it sure was! When I landed at Heathrow airport I was welcomed by the husband, Graeme. Beryl, his wife, had stayed at home.

It was amazing being in the UK although one thing I remember is that I really missed the food from home. I was shown around and visited so many different places, it was incredible, I honestly couldn't believe that I had made it to England. This was a dream that had seemed impossible for a girl like me to achieve, but there I was, living the dream!

I stayed for three weeks before returning to my country and I felt excited to go back because it suddenly seemed like nothing was impossible. I was hoping that I would be allowed to visit my home village to see my little brother and Grandma. It had been six years since I had last seen them and I really wanted to tell them all about England, but when I got back to the orphanage things didn't go very well. During my stay in England, I had spoken to the family about everything that was happening in the orphanage, including the way I was being treated. I never for one minute imagined that Graeme would take it any further, but he did. He had written an email challenging the orphanage about the corruption, so just a few days after I arrived home there was a meeting where I was interrogated about it. I couldn't deny it because it could only have been me – I was the only one from the orphanage to have stayed with this family. I was severely punished, my allowance money was cut, I had to work more in the fields, and I wasn't allowed to leave the orphanage for a few weeks.

That bit of happiness, the feeling that nothing was impossible quickly disappeared. The village father was not happy with me, and I became scared of him. It wasn't because I thought he would physically do anything to me, but his words were painful. He told me that I should be careful because I was the one whose father was in a graveyard. He said that his children had a father and a mother, but I was an orphan and needed the orphanage to look after me. Everything was sour. I would change direction if I saw him coming towards me and I spent a lot of my time and energy hiding away from him. I was sad and lonely.

One day the village father decided to send me to another school. I was told that this had never happened before in the history of the orphanage – I was the first child to be sent away to another school outside of the orphanage and the school he wanted me to go to was about an hour and half's walk away, there and back. Most people said nothing, however the education director fought for me. She told the village father that it was unfair to make me go and study somewhere else when the orphanage had the best facilities and it was unfair to expect me to walk all the way to this other school every day, but he had made up his mind and wasn't going to be persuaded otherwise. The walk didn't bother me because I had grown up walking far to get to school but I felt sad knowing that it was personal, that I was being sent away just so that the village father could get me out of his sight each day.

The education director offered to find me a boarding school and she managed to find me a girl's catholic secondary school, so I packed my things and left for my new abode at the age of fifteen. It was a very strict school, but I managed to get on with a couple of girls who were two classes above me. They kept an eye on me, and no-one bullied me because these girls were well-known and quite tough. All I needed to do was to let them come to my room and share my food with them, which was not a problem as the education director was delivering plenty to me. She became responsible for me when I left the orphanage, and it was great to finally not have to worry about having enough groceries.

During all this I received a letter from Graeme and Beryl. They said they had found me a college that they thought I would like and they invited me to go to the UK to live with them and study. A lot of the people in charge at the orphanage were against the idea, but the education director knew that they were not thinking of me or what would be good for me, so once again she fought for me. She was sure that this opportunity to leave the orphanage would give me a chance to do well and make something of myself. I can remember she used to tell me that I was an intelligent girl, but I just didn't believe in myself.

To everyone's surprise, the village father granted me permission to study in the UK and I believe that was God's hand on my life. I was the first child allowed to visit sponsors from the orphanage and now I was leaving so that I could go and study in England! The mother, uncles, aunties and the other children were absolutely amazed. They couldn't believe it. I remember my three friends at the time saying that it was miracle I was allowed to go, they were so happy for me.

Graeme came so that I could travel back to the UK with him. He had something to do at the church, so once he had done that, we headed off together. Everything was agreed and signed by the orphanage and my sponsors, and they became my legal guardians. I was sixteen years old when I left Africa, arriving in England in September 2003.

Settling In

It felt bizarre initially, it had always been a dream to leave the orphanage and it had always felt so far away but now it was happening right in front of my eyes. I was finally closing the chapter of the life I had lived in Africa, and it felt like I was leaving it behind me. I was looking forward to new beginnings although I still worried about my little brother – I had hoped that one day we would meet again. But overall, I felt happy and hopeful for the future; I felt great! I was introduced to the Graeme and Beryl's two children – Andrew who was married to Diane and in his early thirties, and Duncan who was a few years younger. I was described as the boys' new little sister; I was welcomed in and now I was officially part of their family. They had both moved out of the home, so I didn't see them often, but they used to come over sometimes on Sundays for a family meal. I was allowed to call my guardians 'Mum' and 'Dad', which was a huge step for me as I had never trusted anyone to be a parent to me, apart from my dad. One of my greatest desires was to be part of a family so I felt so happy to have been welcomed into Graeme and Beryl's.

Things were moving so fast. One minute I was in Africa in the orphanage and the next minute, I was here in England, speaking a foreign, broken language surrounded by white people. It seemed like I was the only black person in my new town then, but I know there were others around, I just didn't see them or come across any at the time. It didn't bother me though; in fact, I didn't see myself as being different. I just got involved and got on with life.

At college, things were great! I was studying horticultural and business management and, as the youngest girl on the course, everyone just wanted to look out for me. I spent a lot of time laughing and learning, laughing more though – the guys found it amusing the way I pronounced some of the English words (nothing has changed since then!). Oh it was fun! I spent my time driving tractors, playing football, and working with Nature, which I absolutely loved doing. I was at last being *me* and I was happy. When I was at college my faith was at its strongest, I would say. I totally trusted in God's plan. I remember going to the river near where I lived and just watching the leaves falling into the water during the autumn season in the crisp air... it was magical. I somehow felt closer to my little brother there, as it reminded me of my home village.

I made some great friendships in college, but I spent a lot of time in my room at home. There were not many young people where I lived, and Beryl didn't spend much time with me. For some reason, I didn't feel comfortable around her. I'm incredibly sensitive to tensions around me, and I could sense there was a lot of tension. When I needed underwear and other things, I would ask her if she would take me shopping, but she always sent Graeme instead. I felt like I couldn't say anything because I was in her house, these were her rules that I should abide by.

Just a few weeks after I arrived, Graeme started coming into my bedroom to use the computer – it was in there when I arrived as my room used to be the study. Graeme would not respect my personal space at all – even if he walked in and I was getting dressed, he would just sit there and do whatever he wanted to get done on the computer. I would be struggling, trying to cover myself up as much as I could and get dressed quickly, I felt so frightened. I was too scared to say anything to him or anyone else.

For months, Beryl would continue to send me shopping for personal things with Graeme and he continued to come into my room after I showered. It was beginning to get me down because I didn't know what to do about it. One day, he came in as I was about to get dressed. I was still in my towel so I thought he would leave but he didn't. He sat down at the computer and began to do whatever it was he needed to do. I couldn't take it anymore so I challenged him in the nicest way I could – I had been learning English and the correct way to express myself so I simply said, "Can you leave the room? This is not normal in my culture."

His response was that this *was* normal behaviour in his culture. I didn't know what else to do so I figured I just had to cope with the situation. I began to feel lonely and longed for a close relationship with Beryl so I could open up to her, but that didn't happen.

Five months later, in February 2004, Beryl had something on and had to stay away for the night. Although Graeme made me feel uncomfortable about the 'cultural differences', I trusted him. I think the reason that I trusted him was because he had said to me when I arrived that I was like his own daughter and that he would protect me. I believed him. I believed that he had told me the truth.

Broken

I would normally take the bus to college, but that day Graeme offered to take me there in the morning and at the end of the day he picked me up. On the way home, he drove us to a supermarket to pick up some dinner. He bought steak and chips, and said that it was a treat for us. When we got home, I went into my room while he prepared the dinner.

After we had eaten, he put on a film about King David which I had never seen before. It was about the time David sent his soldier Uriah to war to be killed so that he could have Uriah's wife Bathsheba for himself, after he had committed adultery and slept with her. The film started and it was good. I didn't grow up watching TV and movies, so this was a completely different life and I was curious to learn things. The film was long, but I wanted to watch it. It got to a part in the movie where there was a sexual scene and I became uncomfortable watching it with Graeme, a man I saw as a father, so I asked him to turn it off. But he started to get really emotional, saying how great God was, how amazing it was that God could forgive King David for what he did, how gracious was God. I didn't know how to deal with emotions, so I just sat there feeling very awkward and uncomfortable.

Graeme then moved from the armchair he had been sitting in and came and sat next to me. I was sitting on the bigger couch and he sat right beside me. He took my hand and started stroking it. I thought that this must be another strange English thing that I didn't understand. I assumed that maybe he was comforting me for what he was feeling as he was so emotional. Nothing made sense in my head, but I had never experienced anything like it before. I didn't think or expect anything to happen, I just thought he was very emotional. He carried on talking about God's grace. I remember being so silent, I didn't have anything to say to him, I was just confused at the cultural differences. There were seemed to be so many – I remember being surprised that children could answer back to the older people, whether that was parents, grandparents, or teachers. And the young people would just walk past elderly people without waiting for them to pass first. There was also so much swearing, it seemed to be a 'trend'. Everyone my age swore. These things wouldn't happen back home so it was a huge adjustment.

Something went bang outside. Graeme jumped up and I realised that he had taken his belt off. I didn't question him about this; I assumed that he had eaten too much and it was tight, so he loosened it just as Beryl did when she had eaten a lot. It was a strange thing for me because where I come from, you don't do that in front of people but now, I was in a completely different culture. I felt uncomfortable and confused, so I decided to leave and go up to my room. I was tired from college and I thought that was it. I said, "Goodnight."

Like always, I went to take off my clothes and underwear before putting on clean pants and pyjamas, but I heard the door start to open. Then it stopped. So, I carried on getting ready for bed. Then the door started moving slowly. I was halfway through getting changed so quickly grabbed a red towel which was on the radiator, and wrapped it around me. I turned off the light and jumped into bed. I was looking through under the covers, and I saw him push the door open slowly and come in wearing his dressing gown. He dropped the dressing gown on the floor, and I could see he had nothing on. The room was dark but the streetlights were shining through a little. I was shivering with fear. This was the longest night of my life. I must have gone into shock. I remember he pulled the covers and towel off me and he was on top of me, bouncing up and down saying, "Relax, this can be an enjoyable experience for you."

I remember looking towards the window, and I saw my dad standing there looking very sad. I know this was my imagination, but it gave me a sudden burst of energy and with all my might, I pushed Graeme away and he fell to the floor. He got up and put his robe back on and then he knelt by my bed and started to pray saying, "We mustn't."

He prayed in tongues for a few minutes, then left. I fell asleep not long after; it was like I had passed out. I didn't move or go to the toilet that night. I slept right through the night until morning. I woke up still in shock. I remember I went for a shower and I was in there for a really long time. I was scrubbing myself so hard, I felt unclean; I felt sick to my stomach. After I showered, I was ready for college. I had said nothing to him up to this point. I got dressed and went and sat at the kitchen table for breakfast.

Graeme came in and said good morning as if nothing had happened. I remember answering him with such a broken heart. I honestly thought it would have been better for me to have died that night. While I was at the table, he got up from his chair and stood behind me. Then he put his hands on my shoulders and said that we should not tell anyone about what had happened. He said if we did, that I would get sent back to the orphanage and that I wouldn't want that, because life would be horrible for me again. I didn't have anything to say to him, so I got up and packed my college stuff. He dropped me off at the bus stop so I could catch the college bus.

When I got to college, I really struggled to get through the day. My body was there, but my mind was miles away. I just wanted to cry and talk to someone, but I couldn't. I was so afraid after what he had said and thought that I would get sent back to the orphanage. I didn't want to go back there; I didn't want to miss out on the opportunity it was to be living in the UK. I didn't want to face those smirks from everyone who had said to me that I couldn't achieve anything in my life. My fellow students asked me if I was okay that day. I couldn't tell them the truth; I was in so much pain.

When I got home after college, Beryl had returned. I said, "Hello", and went to my room. From that day I stopped calling them 'Mum' and 'Dad' and instead called them by their Christian names. Beryl never questioned this.

I had thought coming to England was the best thing that could ever happen to me. I had left the past behind to start afresh but instead I was watching my whole world fall apart. It cut me so deep, I can't quite explain it. I hated myself. I hated the fact that I was born. It was such a dark time for me. I felt so lost and lonely. I didn't speak much English so had no way of really expressing my feelings to my friends. I just became very quiet and withdrawn. I saw my dreams and hopes shattered before I had even really started. Just five months after arriving in England and everything had changed in an instant. I began to think about the threat he had put in my head. I comforted myself by believing that this was the price I had to pay in order to have a better life. So, I dusted myself off and got on with life.

One thing that kept me going was the belief that God had brought me out of my home country, across the ocean and into this foreign land for a reason. I saw myself as Joseph who God used greatly after being sold in Egypt. Although I wasn't sold, I related to Joseph who ended up in a foreign land and I knew that God would meet me here and that His plans for me would overcome everything.

"For I know the plans I have for you," declares the Lord,

"plans to prosper you and not to harm you, plans to give you hope and a future.
(Jeremiah 29: 11)

The Religious Spirit

I wasn't coping very well. Although I seemed happy in front of people, I was drowning inside. I was depressed. It felt like I was suffocating. I couldn't breathe to function normally.

My fellow students became more and more concerned about me, so they reported the changes they had noticed to my tutor. One day, the tutor called me to a meeting with him at the college library. He told me that both he and my fellow students had noticed a change in me, and he reassured me that my friends cared about me and that they were all concerned about my welfare. He asked if things were okay at home, if I was happy with my guardians, he asked me if they had hurt me in any way.

My tutor knew Graeme and Beryl and so although I really wanted to tell him how I was hurting, I couldn't because I believed that if I did, I would be sent back to the orphanage. My tutor asked if I needed anything or any help and said that he and my fellow students would be there to support me. I remained silent, terrified the outcome would be me to be sent back home.

In college I put all my energy towards my studies. It kept me going and distracted me each day but when I was at home I was turning into an angry teenage girl. Beryl said nothing. She never questioned why I had become so angry towards her husband. I had lost respect for Graeme, and I didn't feel anything towards her either. Things got really bad, and I remember one day they had an argument. I was in my bedroom, but I could hear him preaching at her that, "he was the head of the family, she had to respect him..."

I got so, so angry, I came out of my room and shouted at him calling him a hypocrite. Beryl got angry with me and told me to apologise. I just walked off and went back to my room. I was hurting so badly; I had never felt like that before. The betrayal was killing me.

I just couldn't understand why he would rape me after knowing everything that had happened to me growing up in Africa. I had told Beryl and Graeme everything – I had been open from the beginning and shared my story with them when I stayed with them during my initial visit to their home. I know the education lady had also told them about what I had suffered, she was so grateful to them for taking me to their home because she saw that getting away from the orphanage and the memories would be good for me and a positive step forward.

I was devastated that Graeme had encouraged me to trust him as a father, that he had asked me to call him 'Dad' and he so often would say that I was like another daughter to him and then he betrayed me and completely took advantage of me. He knew what it meant for me to leave the past behind and to start again in England. He knew that I wasn't a secretive person because I had always been so honest with him and Beryl. I just couldn't get my head around why he would want to hurt me so much. Is that how you treat your children? I was so confused.

I made it through college that term and then I was finished for the summer. To my surprise, I won the 'student of the year' award. As a distraction, a way of not thinking about what had happened, I did spend a lot of time studying and just trying to keep my mind busy. During the summer holidays my guardians decided to take me back to the orphanage and to thank them for looking after me there for so long. I didn't have any desire to go there, but I was looking forward to going back home and this time, no one was going to stop me visiting my little brother and Grandma.

Home

It was July 2004 when we set off for home. Beryl didn't come with us, but Graeme asked his son Duncan to join us. I was happy that I wasn't going to travel alone with Graeme. I just didn't trust him anymore. I don't know if I ever will gain that respect and trust at all.

We left England and I was welcomed back to the orphanage, especially by the children and the education director. I was given a place to stay in one of the visitor's houses and to my surprise, my former youth leader was incredibly happy to see me. The relationship between us wasn't great when I was younger, but on the rare occasion we did laugh together. She was young, late 20s I would guess and had a very fortunate life. Her family were very rich, so I don't think she knew how to relate to us girls in the hostel on a personal level. I felt that she just came into work and did what she had to do – her role involved enforcing punishment when needed, dealing with our allowances and general things like keeping an eye on us.

I felt so happy to be home and one step close to seeing my little brother and Grandma. I remember breathing in and out so deeply to smell the soil and the beautiful flowers. I could even smell the warm heat coming from the ground.

For the first time ever, I was in the guest house all by myself. I had my own space, and it was liberating! I remember just lying on the bed thinking about life, and wondering what my dad would do if he could see me now, all grown up. But what had happened in England, what Graeme had done, still lay heavy on my mind. I couldn't share it with anyone. I had started to think that an orphan like me should expect to be treated like this, I believed that it was a way of paying the family back after they kindly offered to look after me. My own family growing up had treated me terribly too. My uncles would only ever give me a notebook or pencil for school after they had abused me. I was angry with God. I couldn't understand why He allowed this to happen, but I also knew that Satan was the one who comes to kill, steal and destroy (John 10: 10). I knew God wasn't done with me on Earth, and the vision I had of my dad when I was being raped gave me comfort to carry on. I wanted to make him proud and show him that I was okay.

I knew telling people that I trusted could mean that I wouldn't go back to England, and I didn't want to give any reasons to those who didn't believe in me to rejoice in my failings. I was so determined to prove everyone wrong. I was going to fight the pain and return to England to finish my education and become a 'somebody', because I thought at that point in my life that no-one could love a 'nobody'. If anyone told me that I couldn't achieve anything in life, their words would give me a fighting spirit. It was like a burning power and energy would rise up in my belly and I would want to prove the world wrong. It also gave me the challenge to prove to myself that I was capable of achieving something. Since then, God has spoken to me so clearly and I now know that I am dearly loved by Him, that I am significant, I matter, I am enough. I know that God wants to spend time with me and that He enjoys my company. I know now that the one who created me cares for me and that he wants me to live a life in its fullness, a life in abundance, a life of freedom.

A few days after arriving in Africa, we took the children to a nearby lake. We also took a number of mothers, aunties and uncles from the orphanage. I had been working part-time in England, and had saved up some money to pay for the trip. I was also able to bring gifts to the orphans – sweets, underwear and biscuits. We hired a few coaches to take us. I still remember the smiles on those children's faces – it was so beautiful. It gave them a break from their everyday routines which were very restrictive. It was such a treat. It brought a little joy to my soul to see those kids' happy faces. We sang and danced all the way to the lake, and singing those songs reminded me of the time I was in my home village with my little brother. Not so little though, as I was now seventeen years old, he would have been fifteen. He was a young man now, but still my little brother.

When we got to the lake everyone was happy. I remember the children jumping up and down in the water. The colour of the water was phenomenal and the sun was glorious. It was beautiful! I couldn't swim and I was scared of drowning, but I didn't want to have come all this way without embracing that beautiful lake. So, I joined in the fun. I didn't go in too far – I stayed right at the edge of the water. Everyone encouraged me to go in deeper, but I was staying right where I was. I felt safe there.

Duncan offered to teach me how to swim, so I went in a little further with him. I could still stand on the ground where I was, so I was comfortable and I had fun. When everyone started to get tired, we returned back to the orphanage.

Although I had a different guest house to Graeme and Duncan, we ate together. After the lake, I rested and then went over to their guest house for dinner. Duncan sat next to me, and he started touching me and kissing me – I didn't try to stop him. I was a mess, a confused, hurting teenage girl. I wasn't attracted to him in that way. To me, he was my big brother *and* he was in his late twenties, more than a decade older than me. Back home, people would not have approved of a relationship with such a big age gap. But his dad was happy for us. I didn't think anything more of it. I thought that was the end of it.

My Little Brother

The following day, we left for the north in search of my little brother. On our way, we stopped off at my aunty's house. I wanted her to see me now, I was a bit older, to show her that I had moved on. I'm glad we did stop because she told me where my brother was, and she even offered to take us there.

My brother had been taken to the city by a man who had been mending roads in our village. He found my brother just sitting on the road, whilst all the other children were in school. He had been kicked out of the school because the family couldn't afford the school fees – this sadly was quite normal for us; when I lived in the village, my brother and I had to sell maize and bananas to make money for our fees from the age of three. If we didn't have maize or bananas (or sometimes vegetables) we didn't attend school. We missed out a lot most terms, but there was no other way around it.

The man asked my brother why he wasn't in school so my brother told him. He then went on to say he was looking for a chicken to buy for his lunch and my brother told him that Grandma had some and would most likely sell one to him. This kind stranger wanted to help us so my brother took him back home to meet Grandma. As he talked with Grandma, he mentioned a good school in the city and offered to take him and pay the school fees. This was normal to trust a stranger offering help – my region isn't too big and it wasn't busy back then, so everyone knew everyone. And I guess she just hoped for the best for my brother, so he went with the man to the city.

My aunty knew the school he was likely to be attending and this made the search much easier. When we got to the city, the school was closed but luckily there were some students around. They were curious to see us; two white men, a black western-looking girl and my aunty. I introduced myself and told them that I was looking for my brother. They all knew him; he had talked about me with his friends but he wasn't attending school anymore. He now lived with my mum's cousin not far from the school. The man who had brought him to the city could no longer look after him, but my little brother had managed to find a relative to live with instead of going back to the village. One boy who was very fond of my brother knew where the house was, so he took us there. I still remember the excitement on the boy's face – he was so relieved for his friend!

He kept on saying to me, "Your little brother has told me all about you and how you lived in your home village. He knew that one day you would come back for him and bring him an aeroplane!"

I remember laughing and holding back the tears, I had been so scared not knowing if I would find him dead or alive. I remember when my dad died, his brother took my dad's last-born son after the funeral – sadly, he died when he was just two years old due to starvation. So, I was scared for my brother and I remember the walk to the house so clearly. The place wasn't that far from the school, but it felt like an eternity. I felt sick and faint. When we got there, there was no house but a little straw kitchen. I quickly ran towards the kitchen, and at this point my heart was in my mouth and my knees had gone. I saw a boy lying next to the fire looking very weak and very sick. I remember his groaning voice. I called his name.

"It's me, your sister," I said. "I've come home for you."

He got up and ran towards me and we hugged and cried. He said he knew that I would come back for him. The relief I felt was powerful. It was a great feeling! He told me that our mom was back in the village with her husband. He couldn't wait to take me to the village, but we had to go and buy some medicine first as he was sick with malaria. He didn't seem to mind, the adrenaline was pumping for him, but we could all see that he needed food and medical care. My mom's cousin, who my brother had been staying with, wasn't around, so before we left, we wrote a note telling her that I had come for my brother and we had gone to Grandma's together.

When we got to the village, my brother went to Grandma's house and let her know that I was back in the country. My aunty took us to my father's side of the family. My dad's mother was still living there, so we stayed the night. I didn't like being in her company – from a young age I picked up and uneasy atmosphere around her. I was told that she often went to see witchdoctors, and this made me feel scared but I really didn't know her. I have been told that she loved me dearly and was a very kind lady. She apparently got on so well with my mom's mother.

I didn't sleep very well at my father's house. I just wanted to go and be with my brother and Grandma. I couldn't wait for the morning to come. In the morning we left straight after breakfast to go and see my grandma and little brother. It was hard being separated from him that night, but I was scared of going against my aunt. It was her decision and I had to obey it. When we got there, a woman came running down the valley from Grandma's house shouting: "My daughter! My daughter!"

She wrapped her arms around me. I didn't know how to respond to that, but thankfully I was quickly surrounded by other people including my brother and Grandma. We danced and sang lots of songs! One of the songs was *'Yesu ndimuwemi'*, which means 'God is good'.

Titemwa nenge tose ise ndise wana winu,
imwe ndimwe fumu yithu yesu ndimuwemi.

Chorus

Yesu wangazgora suzgo lithu, wangazgora nyengo yamulenji,
wangazgora nyengo ya Muhanya, wangazgora namise wuwo Yesu
ndimuwemi.
Mundigowokere dada ise ndise wana winu, imwe ndimwe fumu
yithu. Yesu ndimuwemi.

I was so overwhelmed but at the same time, I was so happy to see everyone again, including my mother. It was wonderful. The whole village and the surrounding neighbourhood came together to celebrate my return, it was like they had seen a miracle. A girl who had one day just vanished from the village, taken away from my people nearly ten years earlier, and there I was, standing right in front of them in the flesh. I remember those who knew me were touching my face again and again in disbelief. My grandma to this day still looks at me with that look. I don't think she has made sense of things yet.

After lunch, we left for a nearby national park we had planned to visit while we were there. It was good to get away for a bit. Although I wasn't comfortable being around Graeme, I felt safe going to the park with him because Duncan was there and we also invited one of the guys from the city to come with us. I had tried so hard to bury the pain of being raped by Graeme, so to a certain degree, I could cope and deal with meeting my mother and everything that was going on around me. The park was beautiful. We stayed for three days and then returned to the village.

Everyone was commenting on how I had grown and how well I looked, I just responded with a thank you. I talked a little bit about England but everyone seemed to be more interested in the plane and how it could stay up in the air, they saw that as a miracle of its own! They didn't understand the technology of it.

Graeme and my aunt had arranged overnight prayers so the whole village came, but I just sat in the background. My aunt and Graeme were at the centre of attention; they are both very outgoing and outspoken people and it made it easy for me to retreat and not say much. The two uncles who had raped me as a child were there and I didn't know how to handle that, I felt overwhelmed by the emotions but I couldn't express it... being in the same space as these men who had abused and betrayed me was so tremendously difficult. I spent more time with Duncan because although we had kissed, I saw him as a brother and felt safe around him. He continued to treat me more like a girlfriend and I was so confused I didn't stop him. I didn't know what to do.

During the visit, I spent as much time as possible with my brother and Grandma. Graeme offered to pay for my brother to finish school so we took him back to the city and arranged to get a better place for him to stay. We also made an agreement with the headteacher, who said he would look out for him. Graeme paid the fees that were owing so that he could start school again straight away and then we returned to England.

I was comforted knowing that my brother was now okay and I knew that I would be able to stay in touch. I remember thanking God for reuniting me with my little brother and prayed that He would keep him safe. At that point, I had given up on any hope of being happy myself, I had almost surrendered myself to accepting abuse from people. I remember having a lot of conversations with God about how unfair it was to have introduced me to my dad who was amazing and then to take him away from me. I thought God was mean, I didn't understand how He could keep telling me He loved me and then sit back and watch me suffer. Now, as I look through dreams and visions, I can see the Truth. I know that God never tired, that He was always there for me, that He also was hurting for me, that He was holding me so tight. Even when the devil tried to destroy me, God had his hand over my life. I now know that, and I am confident that God has got me.

Dating

I went back to college for the new term, in September 2004. I had been in England for nearly a year now and the reality of what Graeme, my so-called 'guardian' had done, was kicking in. My relationship with Beryl became more and more difficult. Within weeks I found myself in a dark place. I asked them if I could move out as I was working part-time and had found a room in a house-share. Unfortunately, although I could pay the rent, I didn't have enough to cover the bills and neither did Graeme and Beryl. It was cheaper for me to stay with them.

Just a few weeks after returning from Africa, Duncan asked me out. To be honest, it gave me something else to focus on. We went out once and started sleeping together straight away. I wasn't happy having sex before marriage; it was against my upbringing. My past sexual abuse had completely destroyed me – I didn't know what to do, what was normal or how to be intimate with someone. To make things worse, I could see Graeme's face every time I was having sex with his son. The impact was overwhelming and it affected our relationship hugely. I felt sad for Duncan but he was very sexually active and didn't seem to respect my feelings or beliefs... he continued to have sex with me.

Not long after we got together, Duncan invited his grandad out for a Sunday meal at the pub to introduce me to him as his girlfriend. I had already met him but had previously been introduced to him as a member of a family. When Duncan told him that we were going out as a couple he said, "Why on Earth would you want to do that?" He believed I wasn't good enough for his grandson because of the colour of my skin. His family made excuses for him, saying that it was because he was born during the time when black people were seen as slaves, yet they insisted he had accepted me. His comments left me feeling devastated, but because I didn't know my worth I stayed with Duncan.

Everything was moving so fast. We had talked about getting married and Duncan took me to the shop to choose a ring. He tried to take me on a surprise holiday to Amsterdam, but I needed a visa so I couldn't go. Instead, we stayed in a B&B for the night. I knew he was going to propose but in the evening he just went to sleep, so I asked him – I felt so uncomfortable sleeping with him outside of marriage, it was going completely against my culture and beliefs. He sat up in bed, gave me the ring and that was that. We planned to get married once my studies were finished in November.

I was pregnant by April 2005, just seven months into the relationship. I don't remember how I felt about it, but I told his parents. When they found out, Beryl didn't say much to me but Graeme suggested that we should get married sooner. He said he didn't want the church to find out that I was pregnant before marriage, that it wasn't a good example for a Christian family. I remember thinking it seemed more likely his pride would be hurt rather than anything else – his son had impregnated me out of wedlock, I think he was worried about his own reputation.

He called a friend of his at church and asked if there was any space to get married in July. Graeme told this friend that we were crazy in love and we couldn't wait to get married, but this was a lie. Duncan agreed to it, even though he wasn't sure he wanted to even get engaged and they arranged everything over the phone. I had never dreamed of my wedding day like I hear the women say in this country. I had only ever had people tell me that I had no future and that I would marry a man with many wives and children.

The next day, at college, I told my friends that I was getting married. I hadn't told them about the engagement because I felt so young, but I had to tell them because it meant I would be getting married before finishing college. They were absolutely mortified for me. Not only was I getting married at the age of eighteen to someone more than a decade older than me and who I saw as a brother, but I was also pregnant. They didn't believe that I knew what I was doing, and they thought I didn't understand the commitment I was about to make. I remember my tutor telling me that I didn't need to get married. My friends told me that *these people,* i.e., my so-called guardians, were supposed to be caring for me, being a protective family to me and not arranging my marriage to their son. But I was pregnant now and I just needed to do what I thought was best for the baby.

I continued to mentally struggle with what Graeme had done, while everyone was sorting out the wedding, I became more and more angry about what had happened. I began to ask Duncan and Beryl a lot of questions about the family relationships, because it just didn't seem right to me; the way they spoke to each other and the tensions between them. I wanted them to ask me why I had so many questions about Graeme so I could tell them what he had done. But Beryl gave me ridiculous excuses, and Duncan said that maybe his dad had had an affair many years ago which caused his parents' relationship to fracture and for him to become even closer to his brother, Andrew. I later found out that there was an affair which Beryl struggled to recover from.

When I initially came to live with them, Graeme hadn't told his sons that I was going to be joining the family so it was a huge shock for them. They were all still recovering and trying to cope with the aftermath of the affair; they weren't ready to welcome me into their home.

The Wedding

The day came for me to go wedding dress shopping. I wasn't looking forward to it at all. I had been feeling sick from the beginning of my pregnancy, so I had no energy or excitement for it. I think what my college friends and my tutor had said about me being too young to get married played a big part throughout the process. And I also wondered why Duncan didn't want to propose when he deliberately took me away to do so. I questioned everything but I didn't have any answers.

I was expecting Beryl to take me; even though our relationship wasn't great I still thought that she would be the one to take me. Instead, she asked Graeme to. It was mental torture, but I couldn't say anything. He took me to a dress shop where I found a dress. I remember him chatting with the ladies who were helping me to choose one of the dresses. He was telling them how he had gone to Africa and found me in an orphanage and brought me back to England – he had a habit of sharing this story and it made me so uncomfortable, I didn't want everyone knowing my life story.

Everything was in slow-motion for me. I just wanted to get out and go home. The shop was extremely hot and I felt so nauseous. But most of all, I was hurting – my so-called guardians had agreed to care for me, protect me and make decisions in my best interests and this couldn't be further from the truth. I was so confused as to why I was marrying into the family when I had no relationship with them.

I tried a dress on and it was beautiful. I was looking at it in the mirror. Then Graeme asked the ladies if I could come out and show him. I didn't want to but I had to. I couldn't give any reason not to let him see me in the dress. I quickly showed him it and then got changed. It was so hot in the shop; I couldn't wait to get out. It took me less than half an hour to find the dress – I only tried on one dress, and that was the one I picked. We went straight home.

At home, Beryl was sorting out the flowers based on her granddaughter's, Andrew's daughter's, dress. I was grateful but those were not the colours I liked. I wasn't involved much in the planning of my wedding. The venue was chosen by Graeme and Duncan; I was just there to be shown where the wedding reception would take place. I remember seeing the guest list and Duncan made a comment about how it was like his parents were getting married and not us. Most of the guests were his parents' friends and we didn't really know them. I was grateful for what they had done for me and they did ask me if I liked what they had done or were doing, but I would have loved to have been more involved.

Just days before the wedding day, my aunty (my dad's sister) arrived. She noticed that I was very angry towards Graeme. We went on a day trip and again, Beryl didn't come with us but Graeme did. We stopped at a leisure centre to go to the toilet and my aunty pulled me to the side and asked me why I was being so aggressive and why I had a lack of respect for my guardian. I told her then that it was because he had abused me. I hoped she would say that I shouldn't marry Duncan, but instead she told me to forget the past and to get married. She said I had to for the sake of the baby. I told her that I wasn't in love, but she said that I would grow to love my fiancé and I was too young to understand what love was. So, I pulled myself together and carried on, pretending that everything was okay, but I felt like I was slowly dying inside.

The night before the wedding, we went to church for a rehearsal. Beryl stayed home. Graeme wanted to give me away, saying I was like his own daughter and that he was responsible for me. My aunty quickly jumped in and told him that it was not possible for him to do that. They argued so much about it that the vicar had to stop the rehearsal, asking them to take the 'discussion' outside and resolve it. Duncan tried to reason with his dad, but he couldn't; Graeme was adamant. The arguments continued and it was getting late, so I told him to back down. I said to Graeme that if he carried on, he would push my aunty into telling his family what he had done, so he conceded and let her give me away.

After the rehearsal we went home, but Graeme was not happy at all. When we got back, Beryl and Andrew asked why he looked so sad and he told them what had happened. Thankfully and amazingly, both of them agreed and thought it was right for my own family to give me away on my wedding day.

On the morning of my wedding, my aunty was helping to get ready in my bedroom and Graeme decided to come in and use the computer. He found me in a towel, but decided to sit there and do whatever he needed to do at the computer. My aunty was enraged and asked him to leave. He turned around and said that it was normal in England for him to sit there while I was getting ready. She challenged him about our culture and they argued about the cultural differences but then he left the room and I continued to get ready.

I thought a lot about my dad that day. I wondered what he would have said to me. I just wanted to hear his voice, but I knew that was impossible. I was thinking about what had happened at the rehearsal. I wondered if Dad would have allowed the wedding to go ahead if he had found out what Graeme had done. When I was growing up, I had never imagined or dreamed of getting married. I had dreamed of finishing my education and becoming a somebody with a career. I didn't feel very excited, and some of that was because I was nearly five months pregnant and felt constantly sick.

When I got to church and saw my college friends and tutor, I somehow felt okay to get married – their being there felt like a seal of approval. It's like I was constantly looking for someone to say to me that I would be okay and that I was doing the right thing.

After the wedding service we headed off to the hotel reception where there were more photos taken, some food and the wedding speeches – my aunty, Graeme and Duncan spoke, I don't remember much of what was said. We didn't have a first dance, but it didn't bother me. The reception was beautiful, and I felt very grateful. The evening ended with a barbecue at Graeme and Beryl's house.

It was the beginning of married life for me.

You intended to harm me, but God intended it for good to accomplish what is now being done, the saving of many lives.
(Genesis 50: 20)

The Valley

I had found a way of coping with the past, and was carrying on with life, but the hurt and struggles continued. Just a few days after we got married, Duncan told me that a friend of his had said to him on the stag party that black women are just for cleaning your house, not for marrying. I couldn't believe what I was hearing, so I addressed it with the family – they defended him, saying it was "just the way he had been brought up in South Africa", and tried to reassure me. It didn't help, the comments had left a wound and I felt unwanted in the family.

I remember another occasion when I was watching a nature show with Duncan which featured gorillas. He made a comment about how African people look like gorillas; my heart was broken. How could he say that to his wife? When I was at his parents' home, I broke down in tears and told them what he had said, but Duncan just laughed and said it was monkeys, not gorillas. Graeme response was, "ahh that's not too bad...". I felt so alone and so low.

Our son was born just before Christmas – an early baby. In the summer of 2006, we invited my mom and brother over to see the baby. I also wanted to get to know my mom a bit better. When they arrived, it helped to take my mind off things, and I was really happy to have them around. We had a great time together.

When they went back, I slowly began to feel more and more depressed. I was mentally struggling to have a sexual relationship with my husband and I could only respond if I had had some alcohol; most of the time I would just lie there. I couldn't say the word 'sex' for years but because of my upbringing and things I had heard said, I believed I had to fulfil my duties as a wife. Duncan never stopped; he would still have sex with me whenever he wanted, so I saw it as dirty and was disgusted by it.

I continued to feel distant from Beryl and yet I still longed for a closer relationship with her. Although a part of me wanted to talk to her, I didn't trust that she would listen to me. I kept on telling myself that they had brought me here, so I should try and make an effort, so I would invite them for meals in our home but it was such a struggle mentally.

I tried to find a way to tell Duncan what his father had done, but every time I tried to say anything, as soon as I mentioned Graeme's name, Duncan would change the subject or say that he was too tired to talk.

I felt so lonely and lost. I was nineteen years old with a baby and no one to talk to. I had no friends. I stopped attending mother and baby groups. I just wanted to sleep all the time, and do house work when I was awake. I had no relationship with Andrew's wife, my sister-in-law Diane, so I couldn't talk to her either. While all this was going on, I was also dealing with Graeme.

Graeme would come to our house and talk openly to Duncan and I about his sexual relationship with Beryl. I found it hard to process their way of life and I felt trapped. Every time Graeme was in my presence, it reminded me of what he had done and the pain was unbearable. Yet he talked about it as if he had a right to do what he did to me and he would only ever talk about it when we were alone.

One day, he came to our home with a book on forgiveness – the book was written by a lady in America, and it was about how she had been abused by her father and how she had forgiven him. I remember this made me so angry and I threw the book in the bin after he left.

The mental torment didn't end there: Graeme had been given a key to our house when Duncan and his brother owned it, so after we bought the house, Graeme still had a key. He would often pop over to see me on his way into town and if I didn't answer the door, he would let himself in.

I wasn't happy with that. I asked Duncan to take the keys back but he said to me that his father meant well and was just checking I was okay because I had no other family around. Maybe he really believed his dad was trying to help out, but since the rape I couldn't see any goodness in what he was doing.

Just under a year into our marriage, I realised that Duncan wasn't going to stand up for me. I battled mentally through winter but no-one knew that I was struggling. I wanted my husband to talk with me, to listen to me when I tried to have a conversation with him but he would say that I knew when I married him he was a quiet person. I was looking for someone to hear my struggles, even if it was just for five minutes. That was all I was looking for. Yet our conversation was always brief and only ever about what had been happening that day.

I wasn't financially independent in my marriage and we didn't even have a joint account. I had a basic account that I had opened up when I was sixteen, but it didn't have any money in it as I was no longer working. Duncan would give me five or ten pounds once in a while for a bus fare just to get me out of the house. He provided everything but I wanted more freedom financially. He worked full-time and because he was out all day, he would give me his bank card to do the food shopping. I was always so scared that he would get angry if I spent more than the amount he had given me to spend. Every time I went over the budget, I had to call him straight away and tell him before he got home.

Duncan was and still is a great father. He made sure we had everything we needed but I lived in fear because of his anger. It started on our first wedding anniversary – I had cooked us a nice meal and scattered rose petals on the table. He got so angry when he saw it and threw away all the petals. I now know that he was in a lot of financial trouble at the time. He had outbursts of anger and would punch the walls – he put a hole in one of them once, he threw water at me and I just felt afraid of him not knowing when he would flip. He also made me feel like what I had to say didn't really matter because even if we had agreed on something, he would still go to his parents for advice and he would take on board what they had suggested and ditch whatever I had contributed to the conversation.

On one occasion Duncan gave me his card and told me that I could go and buy things for the house. I was excited and fearful at the same time. I went shopping and decided not to be scared so I bought some lamps. As I was walking out of the shop, Duncan rang me. He shouted down the phone at me saying I had spent too much money. I tried to explain that he would like what I had bought and just to wait until he got home to talk about it but he wasn't having that.

He put the phone down on me and rang the shop and had a go at the guy working there. I had to go back to the shop and return the items. The guy didn't like that I had put him in that situation. I apologised to him and he offered me a shop credit note as he said he couldn't do a refund. I took the lamps as there was nothing I could buy from there. I was so embarrassed, I cried so much.

I became pregnant with our second baby in 2007. When I was about five months pregnant, Graeme popped over. It was early in the morning and Duncan had just left for work. I was having a shower when I heard a knock at the door. A few minutes later I heard Graeme's voice; 'Morning!' he shouted up. He must have let himself in. I got out of the shower and went downstairs to see what he wanted. He said he was just passing by on his way into town. I greeted him and told him that I must finish getting ready before my little boy was up, I didn't want to be in his presence for long.

He was about to leave but then he turned around and asked me if he could come back another day to take a picture of me to paint because he said there was nothing more beautiful than a pregnant naked woman. I said, "Goodbye", and ran back upstairs – I was petrified that he was going to hurt me again, but thankfully he left.

When Duncan got home from work, I told him what his father had said. He responded by saying that I was paranoid and that his dad didn't mean any harm. He excused his dad, saying that he was an artist and that is what artists do. I got so angry that I couldn't keep it in anymore – I blurted it all out... that his father had abused me before we got married and that I was mentally struggling with it.

Duncan phoned his father that night and asked him to come over to our house. When he arrived, Duncan asked Graeme if what I had told him was true. Graeme admitted it, and then quickly went on to say that it wasn't dirty because he loved me. I just sat there listening to them. Then Graeme said to Duncan that we needed to manage the situation amongst us because it would destroy Beryl and Andrew if they found out. He said that both himself and Duncan must protect them. My husband agreed to it.

I was lost for words. It confirmed what I was already feeling – I was alone in the marriage, there was no partnership. It killed me. I didn't have any faith in or even respect for Duncan anymore. My fight now was to keep going for my son and the baby I was carrying.

Even though I walk through the darkest valley,
I will fear no evil, for you are with me.
(Psalm 23: 4)

Help

Within weeks after this incident, I got really unwell. I had an ovarian cyst and needed an operation, so I ended up being in hospital for a few days. Duncan would visit me, and during one of his visits Graeme phoned him. I can't explain why, but I completely lost it – Duncan and I got into an argument and although we tried to keep our voices down so no one could hear us, we couldn't. I was so angry with him for not standing up for me after learning what *his* father had done. I think the argument was a cry for help; I wanted someone to hear me so they could find out the truth, which is why I spoke loudly about it to him in the hospital room. I felt so torn because Duncan provided everything for us and he was a good father, but in not fighting for me over his father and his sexual behaviour towards me made me question what kind of a man I was married to.

After my husband left, the nurse walked in. She said that she had heard us arguing and asked me what it was about. She could see that I was upset, so I told her everything that Graeme had done to me. The nurse told me that she had a duty of care and needed to report it to the police. She was also worried because I was pregnant and needed to be protected from any harm. I was so scared, but relieved at the same time. I didn't care about protecting Duncan's mum and brother anymore; no one was there to protect me, and I thought that even if I did get sent back to Africa it would be better than being in the UK and feeling like I did.

I rang Duncan and told him that the nurse knew everything and needed to report it to the police. He was angry but he told me that we would deal with it as there was nothing else to be done now. After I got discharged from the hospital, the police visited us at home. The police officer asked my husband to call Graeme and ask him to come to our house. She spoke to us before he came, and we told the police everything. When Graeme arrived, the police told him what we had said and asked him if it was true. He didn't deny it but said that he was coming from a loving heart and not from the way I saw it.

The police challenged him about his thoughts on what he had done. They confronted him on how he had abused me and betrayed the trust of being my guardian. They talked about my rights to prosecute Graeme if I wanted to. They also told Duncan that his mother and brother deserved to know, but Graeme just said to Duncan what it could do to his mother and brother if they found out. He told me that we could manage it amongst the three of us. Part of me still believed that I should be grateful to them for bringing me to England and paying for my education to give me a better life, so I kept quiet, agreeing to keep the secret from the rest of the family. The police left me a card and said to call if I ever needed to talk or wanted to change my mind about my decision. I so desperately wanted to but the thought of fighting the family terrified me, so I left it.

I tried distracting myself by turning my attention to the garden. It needed a lot of work and as I had a degree in horticulture, I was looking forward to using my skills. I worked right up until our daughter was born at Christmas and it felt good to focus on something else.

Although I still struggled mentally, I wanted to try and make an effort in my marriage. In my culture back home, it is a shameful thing to be divorced. Men don't marry divorcees, especially those with children. My aunt had told me that no matter what, you don't quit in marriage, even if you are being beaten up, it is better to stay married. So one day, I decided to cook us a lovely meal for a date night. I cooked all the time, but this time I made an extra effort. I got the kids ready for bed and made the house beautiful with some nice lights, and I scattered roses all over the dinner table. Duncan got back from work and we sat down for dinner. The evening was going really well, but then our conversation changed; we started arguing about his dad. We both tried so hard to avoid talking about what Graeme had done, but we just couldn't hide away from it. We were being haunted by the past and it wasn't going away. Duncan got upset, he picked up the roses from the table and threw them away and went to bed. I went to bed after him – when I got into bed, he turned me over and had sex with me. He didn't speak and neither did I. This was normal for us; we never spoke before or after sex. It was just a duty that I had to fulfil.

After that evening, I completely shut down. We were both hurting badly and although we were getting on with life, I was just existing. I did my job being a mother and a wife. Duncan's sexual behaviour was eating me away; he would not take no for an answer. We have now spoken about it and neither of us remember having a proper kiss other than a peck on the lips. I felt so low. Lost. Lonely.

One day I decided to just disappear. I didn't want to be home anymore. I got my kids ready and went out. I didn't have any money to catch a bus, so I just walked into town, pushing the double pushchair up and down the streets all day. I didn't have anyone to call or talk to about how I was feeling. When the shops closed at the end of the day, I went to sit in the park. I didn't have a plan; I just didn't want to go home that day. It began to get dark outside and I was worried the kids would get cold, so I walked home. When I got home, I found Duncan and Graeme waiting for me.

Duncan had called his father to tell him I wasn't home. They both knew I was struggling as a result of all that had happened, but they insisted on the secret being kept from everyone else in the family. So whenever something happened, Graeme was the one rushing down to help. That evening he had come to look for me. When I got home and found him there, it made me even more angry. I was at a loss and hurting so much. I didn't know what depression was as I had never heard of it in my country. I felt abandoned by Beryl – I wish she had left me back home, because even though things weren't great in the orphanage I would have been around my people with the same culture and language.

Duncan asked me where I had been, saying he had been worried sick for me and the kids. I told him that I had missed the bus and so I had to wait for the later one. After that Graeme left. Beryl never checked on me after that incident. So I carried on as if everything was okay. I had no choice. My kids kept me going.

Dancing Again

A few months after this incident, two muscular guys turned up at the house. They asked if Duncan was home. I told them that he was at work. One of the guys was trying to explain to me why they were there but I didn't understand what he was trying to say. I stood there looking very stupid. One of them seemed to notice that I didn't have a clue what was going on, plus the baby was crying so he told his friend that they should come back when my husband was home. I rang Duncan and told him what happened. He told me that I needed to start packing because we needed to move out of the house within days. I still did not understand what was going on because he never involved me in the finances. A feeling of protection came over me, and I put the kids in the pushchair and went to the estate agent.

I explained what had just happened, and the owner of the estate agents really wanted to help me. He had just come back from a house which was available and ready to move straight into, so I got my husband to provide everything that was needed over the phone, and we moved a couple of days later. I remember how tired we both were. We moved all night, finally finishing at about five in the morning. Duncan nearly crashed the van at one point – I was supposed to be keeping an eye on him but I couldn't keep my eyes open and fell asleep. He also nodded off and veered off the road, nearly hitting a tree. We both woke up because of the bump and thank God we were okay. I never went back to our old house. My husband told me that the house was taken away from us, and the experience really traumatised me. Not long after that, we both became quite depressed. We were just trying to survive each day, but we put a front on so that no one would know our struggles. What made things worse for me was that Graeme would visit and say things like, "You have to move on from the past", and "I just poked you". It didn't seem to affect Duncan, but I know he was depressed because of the financial struggles. What his father was doing to us was breaking me. I was falling apart.

We moved again to another house just five months into our new home. One day Graeme visited us. I don't remember how they got into this conversation, but Graeme had a way of finding the time and a chance to talk about what he did. He said to Duncan that he understood it was hard for us to cope with what had happened, but that he wanted him to understand that he saw me as a dead rose flower who he was trying to blossom, and that is why he did to me what he did. Duncan looked at me with eyes wide open and said he had just had the revelation of what his dad meant. He said he understood what Graeme was trying to do and what he was saying. I felt physically sick. Things just got really bad from that day.

Duncan's sexual behaviour towards me got worse. Most days I just lay there and thought of my home village or another man I had created in my head just to get me through. I reached out to his mother. Again, I got no response. I tried again and again but nothing. I felt trapped. At this point, I had divorced Duncan in my head. He became just somebody that I used to know. I became so lost that I wasn't functioning properly. One day I was cooking, but my mind was miles away. I accidentally left a tea towel on the gas cooker and went upstairs to do something. The kids were in the lounge and before I knew it, the whole house was covered in smoke. I ran downstairs, grabbed the kids and took them around to our neighbours. I used their phone to call the fire brigade and then went back to the house with my neighbour to try and put the fire out, but the smoke was too thick for us to see anything, so we just waited for the fire brigade. They managed to put the fire out and checked on us to see if we were okay. We then moved to another house in the same town.

I had hit rock bottom but I had to keep going. I reached out to someone I knew well at church and told her about the sex. Her husband spoke to Duncan about it and told him that he would have to take it a step further if my husband didn't stop treating me like that. But nothing changed.

Another time, we had a friend of mine staying with us who had also moved from southern Africa. One evening, towards the end of summer 2011, I asked her if she wanted to go out. I hadn't been out for years! She answered by saying she thought I'd never ask. We laughed so much about it; I remember her saying to me that it was great to see me smile – she was aware of some of the things that I was going through.

We were incredibly excited about going out. I just wanted to dance because I hadn't danced for a long time. We got ready, headed into town and went straight to a nightclub. It was only about nine, so it was quiet, but this was perfect for us because we had all that space to ourselves to dance. We started dancing, but I couldn't move, I had such a heavy heart. My friend encouraged me, but it was not happening, so I decided to sit down and just watched my friend dancing.

I noticed a group of guys walk in, one of them came straight towards me looking very confident. He said, "Hello", in an Irish accent and put his hands out, inviting me to dance. I smiled and said that I didn't know how to, to which he responded that he couldn't either. So, I gave him my hand and we headed to the dance floor. I remember swinging around with so much freedom! I was teaching him how to dance in an African way, and he was teaching me the Irish 'river dance'. I was captivated by his smile and voice. I felt like for the first time ever in my life like I mattered.

I wanted to stay in that moment forever. We danced all night until the club finished at about four in the morning, before we went home.

Attacked

I had exchanged numbers with the Irishman, so the next day I decided to contact him. I couldn't let him think I was interested in him; I was married and needed to let him know. We arranged to meet up the following day, and he picked me up from town and drove me to the beach. It was a beautiful evening; the sky was clear; it was quiet and so peaceful. It felt like everything around me was still, but my mind was travelling at a hundred miles an hour. All I kept thinking about was that although I liked him, I had to tell him that I was married. I kept on telling myself to just get on with it, but I couldn't find the words.

Then suddenly, with such heartache I whispered, "I'm married." It was loud enough for him to hear what I had said, but he just carried on walking. My heart was in my mouth by then. We walked along the beach and sat down near the rocks. He asked me if I loved my husband, so I told him the truth – that I cared a lot for Duncan, but I saw him as a big brother and, for the first time ever, I poured out my heart to this guy I had only just met. I told him everything.

He said something to me which changed my life; "You have a choice in how you want to live your life." Those words spoke so clearly to me that night and I saw a glimmer of hope.

He took me back home and we said goodbye to each other. I thought we would never see each other again, but a few days later I bumped into him again. We became friends and he encouraged me to get a job – he spoke to his dad who was in charge of a company and thankfully there was a job available. They also completely understood my childcare situation and were willing to work around my kids. I was so excited and thought that getting a job would be beneficial for both me and my husband. We had tried so many times to find a job for me but always struggled with childcare, so it was good to work for a company where someone understood and was happy to be flexible.

I was honest with Duncan about how I had met this guy. I had become fearless in those days and was determined to turn things around for us. I even found us some marriage counselling – a church near us was running a course that had just started, so we joined. I was hoping that I might learn to fall in love with my husband, but I remember when we got there, we had a meal and this guy was talking us through a marriage video. We looked around us and saw other couples who seemed a little closer to each other than we were.

I remember walking out of it feeling worse than when I went in. I couldn't even hold hands with my husband. I couldn't tell him that he was a good husband. I had always told him that he was a good father, but to tell him he was a good husband was impossible. The words just wouldn't come out of my mouth. We only attended a couple of times but Duncan got nothing from the counselling and so we decided not to go anymore. We began to argue more and more and grew further apart. The arguments were always about what Graeme had done and I was also resentful towards his mother for bringing me to England but not wanting to have much to do with me.

One evening, Duncan and I had a massive argument about his dad. We tried so hard to leave the past behind, but we couldn't and we said things to each other that were hurtful. Duncan drank a bottle of vodka and went to bed early. I went to my friend's room but couldn't settle, so I went downstairs to watch TV. The Irish guy phoned me – he wanted my address so that his dad could send me the job application forms. He had moved away by then, just a few weeks after I had met him.

Whilst I was on the phone, Duncan came downstairs. He could hear me giving the address and talking about the job. I waved at Duncan as I was on the phone. He walked past me and headed to the kitchen to get a pint of water. He walked through to the lounge as if he was going to pass me, but then he stopped and poured the pint of water on me. He tried to grab my phone but I managed to run to the kitchen. He followed me, so I ran into the dining room but I had nowhere else to go from there. At this point, I had always believed that Duncan wouldn't hurt me, but I was aware of how drunk he was and I knew that it was dangerous for me to trust him in the state he was in, so I went under the table and got out of the house.

My friend was still on the phone and kept saying, "Call the police! Call the police!" It was only then that I realised the phone was still on, but I told my friend that I could sort it out and that he shouldn't call them. Then I hung up.

I had run out of the house without shoes and was only wearing a night dress. It was winter and icy and I was so cold that I decided to go back to the house, but Duncan had locked me out. I walked up and down the housing estate to keep warm, but it was freezing, so I sat on the decking in front of our house. After about forty-five minutes I couldn't feel my fingers. It was at the point that I remembered my girlfriend was staying with us so I rang her, but she didn't pick up the phone. I started throwing stones at her window, but she didn't hear me.

After a while, she turned the main lights on, she must have been going to the toilet, so I decided to throw another stone and this time she heard me. She came downstairs and let me in – she'd been listening to music through her headphones and hadn't heard a thing.

Telling the Truth

I went to bed and Duncan said nothing to me, and I said nothing to him. In the morning, he turned me over and had sex then left for work. This sexual behaviour was normal in our marriage. I became like a robot in our marriage, just letting him get on with it. That morning, I watched him go to work and then I got up, showered and got the kids ready.

At this point, I would have normally called him to ask if he was safely at work and apologise to him after the previous night's argument. I apologised every time we had an argument. I wanted us to sort things out and to start again. This time it was different. I didn't call. I didn't want to check on him because I was hurting so much. I knew that we needed help, so I decided to reach out to his parents.

When I called, Beryl picked up the phone. She said, "Hello?", then passed the phone to Graeme when she heard it was me. She would do this whenever I called. Before I even began to speak, Graeme told me that I had been asking for what Duncan had done to me, that I shouldn't have been speaking to another man because I was a married woman. I felt so angry. I had this pain that was choking me. I hung up the phone and rang my pastor instead, he advised me to stay with a friend for a few days as it wasn't safe for both me and my husband to be in the same house and to be so angry with each other.

I made some phone calls and a couple I knew were happy for me and the kids to stay with them. After a few days we returned home and tried to talk things through. We tried to get on with life, but we were two very broken people. Just days after the incident, another couple invited us to their house for a meal. They asked Duncan what was going on as they had seen me emotionally deteriorate so quickly. Despite everything I was going through at home, I was always trying to be brave and happy, so people saw me as a strong and cheerful woman on the outside. When I could no longer put on my 'happy face', my friends saw a change in me and were worried. Duncan broke down and told them everything that we were going through, including what his dad had done.

After telling them, Duncan took me to his mother and brother and told them too. He said to me that we couldn't carry on like this, and I was so relieved. Finally, we could get help! I had given up the idea of getting a job by this point, as I felt I had to sort out what was going on at home first. I actually thought our marriage now had a chance of surviving. Graeme was abroad when we went to tell Beryl and Andrew. The family said we would get through this together, and that they were sorry I had been through so much. I felt like there was a breakthrough.

Our family (including Graeme and Beryl) all attended the same church, so the pastor felt it was best to support us all. Beryl was very emotional and grateful for the support from our pastor and his wife, but it didn't last long. A few days after Graeme returned home, the pastor and his wife visited them to talk and try and find a way to move forward. He also asked Graeme and Beryl to stop going to our church, so that I could have space to heal and get help. The mood changed and Beryl became protective over Graeme and asked my pastor and his wife to leave.

Things changed for the worse. The family ganged up against me, saying that I should be able to move on from the past. We began to fight, back and forth. My pastor tried to talk with Duncan, but he wasn't listening, he didn't want to hear his dad being accused of rape. One day Andrew's wife, Diane, rang me and asked if we could meet up. This gave me a little bit of hope, I thought she wanted to help me, to move forwards and I began to dream that we would all get through this and that everyone was just hurting but it would be okay. A few days before Christmas, Duncan drove me and the kids to Andrew and Diane's, but on our way there she phoned. She told Duncan that she didn't want to see me, but was happy to see him and the kids. I was devastated. I had been so looking forward to finally beginning to build a relationship with her, but she said she thought she was ready, and could cope with a visit, but she couldn't. Duncan dropped me off at the bus stop and he took the kids to see their uncle, aunt and cousins. He left them there, and came back to the bus stop to take me home. I told Duncan that if it had been my brother or family member who had said that to me that I would have told them I was going to take my family back home and that we would go when they were ready to see us all together.

Darkness Will
Not Overcome

I had become so sad and lonely, I began to feel suicidal. My children were only four and six, and I didn't want to leave them, so I tried so hard to fight my emotions. But everything had become so dark. I told myself that the kids would be all right, that they had a father who loved them. Because I wasn't just fighting my husband but his family too, it finally got too much. One day in October, I took an overdose.

It was late afternoon when I took the overdose. I was hoping to just slip away in my sleep, so I went to bed as usual but at midnight I woke up with my heart racing, like it was going a hundred miles an hour. I told Duncan what I had done and he dialled 999. I was rushed to hospital and I remember lying there having given up the fight. I couldn't see properly because of the drugs; I just saw shadows of people but I could hear them talking. The doctors told Duncan that I had damaged my liver, and they were planning the next step. They were thinking of transferring me to another hospital, just in case my liver gave up. Duncan had to take the kids home, and I remember one doctor saying to me that they were trying their very best to pump medical charcoal into my body, but he was worried because of the amount of overdose that I had taken and the time it took for me to be taken to the hospital.

My pastor visited that day. He sat by my bedside and started to pray. I couldn't see him properly, but I recognised his voice. As he was praying, he wept for me with such a sad voice. I was suddenly filled with a desire, deep inside of me, to fight for my life. I remember just repenting for what I had done, for what I had tried to do, and I asked God to give me another chance. Then my pastor left. That evening, Duncan returned to the hospital. The doctors told him I was going to be okay because my liver had begun to repair itself. I was discharged from the hospital a few days later and I could see how my decision to take an overdose had affected Duncan. But I was numb to any feelings. I didn't matter anymore. The only thing that mattered now was that my kids were okay and I was going to be around for them.

Within a few days of being home from the hospital, social services came to visit me. When they found out the reason for my attempted suicide, they contacted the police to discuss the case we had raised back in 2007. Social services then began to work with us to find a healthy and safe way forward, but Duncan began to fight me. He wanted me to tell social services that I was okay and that his father had just made a mistake, but I couldn't. It still didn't make sense to me why he and his family couldn't recognise or understand that what Graeme had done to me was so devastating. In every meeting with social services, Duncan and his family fought me. I asked my pastor and one of the female leaders at church to attend the meetings for some support. I felt I had no one on my side, no one helping me and I was exhausted.

The family all had their reasons for their actions; Graeme told social services that the night of the attack, he was too hot, which is why he took off his clothes. He said it wasn't because he had planned to abuse me, and his family agreed with him saying that they didn't see what he had done as rape. Beryl said she had never been in agreement about bringing me from Africa to England, that it had been Graeme's idea and she just went along with it. She said she was going through "her own stuff" when I moved in with them and that was why she couldn't be there for me. Duncan and his family told social services that I was mentally ill and that I had blamed all the abuse that had happened to me in Africa on my husband and his father. My pastor and his wife stepped in and fought for me on that allegation. Social services asked me to get a note from the doctor saying that I was mentally well and could keep my children. Thankfully, the doctor gave me this letter and I was allowed to keep the kids in my care.

The family continued to tell me that I should have moved on from what had happened to me, that I should be grateful for the education they had provided for me and my brother, that they had given us a better life. To me, it had been years of trauma. After hearing what Beryl had said, I became so angry with her, feeling let down by my supposed guardian, it felt like I had been thrown into the lions' den to be devoured.

The police advised me again that I could still press charges against Graeme, but I was so physically and mentally drained and I couldn't fight the family. Although I had my pastor and my friend during the meeting, I still went home alone with my husband. Graeme didn't deny what he had done, he only made excuses about it and so the police decided to charge him. They could see the facts – he was my legal guardian, he betrayed trust and so was cautioned and was put on the sex offenders register. This didn't go down well with the family, and Duncan and I argued about it daily after this decision was made. He wanted me to convince the social services and the police that Graeme didn't mean to hurt me and that he wasn't who the police thought he was. I felt so sad that Duncan was so blind to see the pain his father had caused me, and I just didn't understand the family's thinking, that they couldn't see that as rape.

I began to think of my future and my kids. I thought a lot about what my friend had said that night on the beach, that I had a choice about how I wanted to live my life and I began to imagine a life outside of the marriage. I began to think about where I could be in ten years' time and I started to see a glimpse of hope for the future. I found myself at a crossroads, wondering which road to take. I remembered the freedom I felt when I met my friend and the feelings I had back on the beach, the excitement of finding someone who liked me, who was kind and interested in who I was. I imagined what was it was like to fall in love and to be in love.

Soon after Christmas, I told Duncan that I wanted a divorce. He was shocked and heartbroken. He rang his parents and they tried to talk to me out of it, but all I could think about was what my friend had said; that I had a choice about how I wanted to live my life. And I was *so* unhappy with the life I was living. My pastor supported my decision and within a month I had left my husband and moved into a new flat with my kids.

Starting Over

I continued to meet with social services, and I started attending a victim support group. Six months later, I moved to another town and started to take positive steps forward: I got two jobs, working both at the weekends and in the evenings; I went back to college and trained to become a beauty therapist; and I had driving lessons. Duncan and his family did not stop fighting me, but my pastor stood by me all the way.

One day, Duncan came to my house to see the kids and he took them out for the day. When he came back, he wouldn't leave my house. This was my battle with him. He didn't accept our break-up, and still wanted to treat me like his wife. So many times I felt like giving in for the sake of peace but I kept remembering what my friend had told me on the beach – I had a choice. So, I just took life one day at a time, always pushing forwards. The day he wouldn't leave my house we argued so much. I put the kids to bed and then went to bed myself, he just wouldn't leave and there was nothing else I could do, so I left him in the lounge. I could see he loved our kids, but he didn't seem to care about me. I didn't want to go back, I wanted to move on, maybe to even fall in love one day. While I was upstairs, I could hear him crying in the living room but I stayed where I was. I couldn't get back together with him, I just couldn't. Love protects, and he only ever tried to protect his parents, not me. It got so late that I eventually fell asleep. When I woke up it was about one in the morning and I could hear the sound of two voices – Duncan was downstairs talking to his dad! He had rung his mother and she had sent Graeme over. They wanted to 'talk some sense into me'.

Duncan and Graeme came upstairs and into my bedroom, and stood at the foot of my bed. Duncan cried, while Graeme told me off for being stubborn. He was praying for me, telling me that I had demons in me and that my ancestors did not like me being married to his son, and that they were calling me back home. Graeme said he wanted to fight these demons so that I could get back together with his son. I just sat in bed shocked, I didn't know what to do. They eventually left the house sometime after two and I managed to get a few hours' sleep but then I had to get up and take the kids to school. All I wanted to do was keep my kids home and sleep. I was physically and mentally exhausted, but I pushed myself to get ready for school, I thought at least that way I could rest whilst they were out.

On the school run, a friend I had just met saw that I looked tired and invited me to her house with her husband. I told them why I was so tired, and she offered to call the police so that they could explain my rights as someone living in the UK. They could see that I was still trying to protect Duncan and his family – even at this point I felt like I should be grateful that they had brought me to the UK, but I agreed to them calling the police. I had had enough and when they came, I told them what had been happening. The police explained everything to me, including my human rights in this country, so when I left their home, I walked straight into town and to the Courts of Justice. I was so angry and I wanted to change my surname for my sake and my father's. I marched through the court gate looking and feeling furious and went to a small window where I told the man behind the desk that I wanted a divorce. My heart was pounding. He directed me to the solicitors' office, which was just down the road, and when I arrived there was a lovely lady who worked with me. The divorce went through very quickly after that because of the terms and conditions I had filed the divorce on.

My pastor and the lady who had attended previous social services meetings supported me. When the divorce papers came through and had to be signed, I was so scared that Duncan would fight me on the grounds that I had filed for divorce, but I was ready and willing to fight back. I had friends who had witnessed and challenged Duncan's behaviour so many times throughout our marriage that I knew I would win the case if we had to go to court. I prayed for a miracle. Duncan was very angry when he received the papers, but he signed them. I remember the feeling when I got the phone call from my solicitor to tell me that he had signed the papers – I still remember the relief! It was so overwhelming that I cried and laughed and was scared all at the same time, but I knew where I was going was more promising than where I had been. I remember dancing and singing in my home language. That's one of the things I am best at – when I dance, I lose myself in it, I'm no longer in this world, I'm in a different place.

I finished my studies and became a spa therapist. I passed my driving test which gave me more freedom to get around. It has been a long and challenging journey, but because of my faith in Christ, I have been able to forgive and to be free from the pain I carried for years. My journey in life has taught me to become the person I am today. My relationship with the family is not without its challenges, but we are all trying our best for the sake of the children and so that everyone can get on with their own lives. These relationships can't go back to how they were.

It has taken me time, but I now know that what happened to me wasn't right. No one should have to go through that. It is wrong. Although I have had some sort of apology, I am aware of the tensions that still exist. I guess time is a healer and faith plays a big part in that process.

Healing

It has been such a journey of healing and forgiveness. When writing this book, I had so many moments with God, so many dreams, visions, wakings and it has been healing to journey through my life with Daddy by my side. I want to share what the Lord said to me during this time.

June 8ᵗʰ 2020

I woke up crying uncontrollably. I had been talking to God about things, and He has revealed some of the reasons for the pain I suffered. He showed me that when Dad's children rejected me in the orphanage it hurt me much deeper than I thought. I felt lost. Dad's death left a deep void inside me for years. I hadn't come to terms with the reality that he was gone. The Lord showed me that my healing began when I cried out to him to take away the anguish and pain I was suffering. He showed me that when Dad died, I was suffocating, choking, and drowning in pain. But the Lord was always by my side waiting for me to call out to Him, to ask Abba Daddy to help me. And that's what I did in Israel in September 2019. God has promised that I'll continue to go through the process of healing, but He has taken the deep aching pain away from me. I can now breathe in and breathe out.

God has also reminded me of a word my pastor gave me at the River Jordan during my rededication. God has also shown me that I struggle to relate to my mum because I don't know her, but that loving her because she gave birth to us is enough.

These are the words that God has given me about my ex-husband wanting sex as he did – no one should be worrying about fulfilling their other half's sexual needs all the time. But I did. And it's not okay. No one should have to go through that. Even if it comes from a loving place, it's not okay. I hope that by speaking up about this someone in a similar situation might be freed from this lie.

I want to focus on how faithful God is and how he has carried me all through it all. I am here, free of HIV and Aids and mentally stable because He knows my name. Because I am His. Because He loves me. Because He cares. Because I matter to Him. Because He wants me to live a life in abundance. Because I am one of His sheep and Jesus is my shepherd. Only because of God can I sing a new song today.

I have completely forgiven those who have hurt me because I want to be free and to love unconditionally. I know that this is what God would want me to do. What happened is not okay. No one should have to experience that, but no matter what, I want to live a life in forgiveness and love because that's how I fight my battles. I don't have to live in bondages because of the past. The future is as bright as I want it to be. And with God in it then I'm unstoppable. I can fly and be free.

Free as a Bird

As for me, love hasn't happened yet, but I am pressing on and looking forward to the future's adventures. I had thought that one day I would write my story, but I never thought it would actually happen. I am not a writer, I'm not very good at sitting still, I always have to be 'doing' something, but this wouldn't involve writing. Essays were my worst nightmare in school but during the recent lockdown due to the global pandemic, I felt strongly that I should sit down and write. So here I am, sitting in my lounge writing my story.

One of the reasons I am writing my story is not to dwell on the past, but so that I can look back through my life and learn from my mistakes and the mistakes of others. I know I made many mistakes along the way! I also want to try to understand what was going on inside me during all those years so that I can become a better me. My hope is that lessons have been learnt from these experiences. I hope that if anyone gets the chance to read my story, they will be able to see beyond the struggles and find the hope amongst the chaos. I hope that people will be empowered to know that we all have a choice in life to live the best life we can. Everyone deserves that. We just need to choose which path to take when we find ourselves at the crossroads. No matter how uncertain things get, there is always hope.

When I was younger, I never properly cried. The day my father died, he cried over me. I still remember his strength when he was holding me, and squeezed me in his arms crying, 'My child, my child,' before he took his last breath and his sister and mother took me away from him. His sad voice has stayed with me all these years and I have held back the tears because I didn't want my father to know that I was hurting. I wanted to be strong for him, even when I have been choking with grief. When the world asked if I was okay, I had no other response than to say, 'I am okay, it's okay, it's fine'. I didn't know how to express myself.

This book has helped me to tell the world how I have been feeling. This book has allowed me to cry. I have been rejected by my father's family and the pain of this had a horrible effect on me. I have been searching for somewhere to belong over the years, but because of Jesus I have found a place that I can call home. I find comfort in what Jesus did on the cross. Knowing His love, I know I belong. I love these bible verses:

'Defend the weak and the fatherless, uphold the cause of the poor and the oppressed. Rescue the weak and needy, deliver them from the hands of the wicked.'
(Psalm 82: 3-4)

'A father to the fatherless, a defender of the widows is God in His holy dwelling.'
(Psalm 68: 5)

116

Dreams and Visions

I was twelve years old when I had my first vision. God has spoken to me so much over the years through dreams and visions, so I wanted to include them here. If anyone is going through anything even slightly similar, I want to reassure you that God cares so much about you. No one deserves to be treated the way that I was, and I know that this isn't a reflection of God's love for me. The dreams and visions were powerful, tangible moments where I experienced God in an incredibly beautiful way. I pray that whatever trial you are in, you will know the comfort of God, you will hear Him whisper and see Him in dreams. If He is for us, who can be against us? **(Romans 8: 31).**

The vision.

I have already mentioned the first vision I had when I was twelve years old – it was when I became very sick in the orphanage and was rushed to hospital. Before the operation, my doctor prayed for me. During the operation I went to another place, so I didn't wake up at the time they were expecting me to.

I saw myself in a coffin made of ice, and I could see right through it. I was surrounded by a beautiful ice floor; it was so peaceful. As I looked a little further, I saw a man wearing a robe. I said to him, "I know you", he smiled and said, "Come closer, look where the nails went into my feet. And see my hand, where the nails went in." I looked and saw holes on his feet and hands. I jumped with excitement, "Yes, I know you! You're Jesus!" He smiled and said, "Go back little girl," and I woke up coughing, surrounded by a team of nurses and doctors.

November 2001 – a dream.

In my dream, I saw a beautiful city all lit up. As I walked through the city, I felt the presence of the Lord around me. There was unbelievable peace there, it was so overwhelming. I felt I belonged there and I heard the Lord say to me that this was my home.

November 2001 – a dream.

A few days after this dream, I had another. I saw a mighty hand across my bedroom and then heard a voice calling my name. The voice echoed through the whole room. It felt like I was surrounded by thunder! My bed shook so much I was terrified and I woke up sweating and shaking. I knew it was the hand of my Holy God.

Another dream.

I saw Jesus as a shepherd with lots of sheep standing in a very green and lush field. A sheep wandered off to the cliff edge, and Jesus followed it and brought it back to safety.

Summer 2009.

I went on a retreat with the church. We were in beautiful surrounds, and we were shown around the area. As I went over a bridge with the river running underneath, I stopped to have a look. I was blown away by the beauty which was all around me. I watched the leaves falling into the river, then coming under the bridge to the other side. I began to talk to God about things. I asked Him how was it fair to punish those who have never before heard the name of Jesus because of their culture or where their homeland is? I thought about those who live in the forest or rural areas that can't always be reached. The Lord answered me and said that His existence is all around us, His presence is everywhere. He is in all creation because He is THE creator. This was a hard truth to swallow.

Autumn 2009 – vision.

During the prayer meetings on the retreat, someone was praying for me. I felt a burning fire going through my entire body. Then, I saw a raging sea, above which was a dove in such stillness. I heard a voice from above say that there will be a time in my life that God would restore peace, joy and laughter. Though the ocean might rage, it would not touch me for He will always be with me. Suddenly, the raging sea became silent and there was a stillness around me. I watched the waves gently rolling on the beach, then drawing back into the sea with a beautiful peaceful sound.

May 2015 – when it seemed like there was no hope.

A friend of mine invited me over for a cup of tea, and she could see that I was worn out and very sad. I went, but all I wanted to do was go home and sleep. I sat at the table and was very quiet. My friend asked if he could pray with me, and as he started to pray, I had a vision – I saw myself and my kids in God's hands. Then the Lord said to me, "I have you and the kids, you are safe and protected in my hands and I am not going to drop you. I am dealing with things in the other family but it's no longer your problem and you can be assured of this."

Then God asked me where my resting place was. I thought it must be in the kitchen because I enjoy cooking. Then I remembered a picture I had seen in a dream many years ago, of a girl running towards God's wide, open arms. Then I realised that God was my resting place, so I told God. He then asked me to sit on His lap, so I did. He asked me if I had ever called Him Daddy... I didn't think I had, although I had called Him 'Abba' and 'Father'. He encouraged me to call Him 'Daddy', so I did, and it felt so good! My face lit up. God asked me what I wanted my daddy to do for me. Straight away I said that I wanted Him to take away the pain and to make everything okay. Then He passed me a box and told me to put all my worries, pain, shame and all that is not good in the box and hand it to Him.

God asked me what else I wanted my daddy to do – I asked for a fulfilled, abundant life. God then asked me what I wanted from Jesus. I looked and saw Jesus sat at the right hand of the Father who was seated on the throne. I told Him that I wanted a restoration of my joy in the Lord, and to smile again. God then asked what I wanted from the Holy Spirit and I could feel the Holy Spirit all around me. I said I wanted the Holy Spirit to go before me in my everyday life and to be my guide, my counsellor and to give me discernment to know good, and what is not of the Lord. After this encounter, things began to change for the better in my life. It was incredible.

May 2015 – worship gathering.

I attended a prayer gathering one weekend, and during it a lady who didn't know me came to pray with me. She began to prophecy over me saying that there would be a river of life running through my life, and that I would share God's goodness. She said that through me, God would heal the broken hearts and I would share the hope of Jesus Christ. She told me that God wanted me to know that the smile He had given me was not to be hidden away.

That evening, someone else had a word for me. They said they felt God had a purpose over my life and, since I was a child, the devil had known about it and tried to destroy it but the devil was fighting a losing battle. This word was also prophesied over me by someone else a few months later.

April 2017.

I had strayed away from church, I knew the danger of staying away from fellowship but I guess I just wanted a bit more freedom in the world. The more I stayed home, the more my spirit was bothered by it. I became more comfortable around friends who used bad language, I found it easier to compromise God's name even when I knew my spirit was not at peace. The more I joined in the things of the world, the more uncomfortable I felt.

One day, I contacted a church leader for personal reasons – I felt comfortable talking to him so I confided in him. He asked me a very personal question and I answered honestly, and he then went on to encourage me to get back into fellowship. After the call, I was fuming. I felt so angry that he had asked me such a personal question, but the Lord was stirring me and I couldn't meet up with those people I had been hanging out with. It got to a point where it felt like the guy was in my house, encouraging me to get back into fellowship that I couldn't ignore it anymore. I went to the church and became part of the family, and I'm loving what God is doing in my life.

April 2019.

I became homeless and ended up staying at work while a friend looked after my kids. One day, I was so exhausted that my boss could see it and told me to finish early. I went to my room and knelt on the floor. I was missing my kids so much and began to cry with such a deep sorrow, I started to pray in tongues uncontrollably and was so exhausted that I fell asleep. I then had a vision of Jesus; He was sitting under a big, beautiful tree, wearing a blue rob with a gold sash around His waist. The grass was unbelievably green; the leaves on the tree so well nourished and healthy looking. I was standing at a distance when Jesus called to me. He invited me to come and sit with Him, to lean on His shoulders. I did and felt so much peace! When I woke up, God led me to Psalm 23 and the next thing I knew my phone was ringing and my friend had felt prompted to share that very same Psalm with me. That was a special day because later on I found a house for me and my kids to move into. Wow, what can I say? God is so good and continues to bless us so much.

September 2019 – Jordan River, Israel.

The Lord said to me, "I am pouring out healing rain over you for your past traumas. I am filling you with the fire of Heaven and the Holy Spirit which I will blow through you and it will extend to others to break chains and strongholds." Then said to me, "Tell the devil to take a seat. He needs a comfortable one because he will be there for a long time. Watch what the Lord is going to do with your life."

During my baptism in the River Jordan, a word was given to me: I will be a victor, not a victim.

February 2020 – a vision.

I saw a field and in it the Lord Jesus was digging up the ground so that the fertile ground could be even. He was also removing the unwanted things from it.

Sow righteousness for yourselves,
reap the fruit of unfailing love,
and break up your unplowed ground;
for it is time to seek the Lord,
until he comes
and showers his righteousness on you.
(Hosea 10: 12)

April 2020 – a dream.

I was standing right in the middle of the world and there was a giant glass which allowed me to see both sides of the world. To my left, there was a very tall, black demonic-looking spirit and he was in charge of the world. I looked around and beyond it and saw beautiful colours which were so attractive and inviting. Then I looked down and saw many holes with vicious fire coming up out of them. That beauty was a trap, drawing people into a place of danger.

Then I looked to my right where I saw trees everywhere. They looked so green, so vibrant in colour and well nourished. As I looked deeper into the trees, I saw the Holy Spirit being poured deep into the trees' roots and overflowing into the leaves. There was a never-ending nourishment for the trees. I felt stillness and a sense of plenty and abundance. It was so calm and peaceful – a paradise.

Printed in Great Britain
by Amazon

38080695R00071